THE BACK

CON HOULIHAN

BOGLARK PRESS

© Con Houlihan 1998
The moral rights of the author have been asserted.

Boglark Press, P.O. Box 1227, Portobello, Dublin 8.

First published 1998

All rights reserved. This book is sold subject to the condition that it shall not, by way of trade or otherwise, be lent, resold, hired out or otherwise circulated without the prior consent of the author/publisher in any form of binding or cover other than that in which it is published and without a similar condition including this condition being imposed on the subsequent publisher.

ISBN 0-9529847-0-9

Printed and bound in Ireland by Harcourt Printing Company Limited

This Book is dedicated
to all people of goodwill
in the New Ireland

CONTENTS

Foreword	1
Introduction	5
Mo and the jungle	7
Ray Wilkins, seventeen years later	10
A great writer in Croke Park	13
Recalling glory at Goodison...	15
Downfall of a hero	18
Bull's eye of the turf	20
From the screen to the green	24
Balgriffin, gateway to lovely links	27
Bicycles rule, not footballs	30
Bogged down in Kerry	33
Winter school	37
The days of port and periwinkles	41
Free enterprise in the turf world	44
The big game – when pressure meant steam	48
'Wicket' season for England	51
Streets broad and narrow	53
Jim Murray sees red	57
The mirage known as fame	60
A change of scenery worked wonders for Hatton's Grace	63
Marathon running is child's play!	66
Stoking up a fond memory	68
Cheltenham revisited	71
Hoary myth is dead	74
Las Vegas in a field near Clondalkin	78
Aficion, a mix of love, expertise	80
Drama In Tokyo	83

Walking tall in the garden	85
Stewards' enquiry at Knocknagoshel	88
Requiem for a friend	92
Rural boys in Chicago	95
Slow Boat To China	98
A Freeman now trapped at home	100
Black humour – Bruno style	103
Lewis still has some way to go	106
How to wren-ch the eagle's glory	108
Joe, Gentle Giant from Tiger Bay	111
Liam made the most of his gifts	113
A wonderful Constitution . . .	116
Much to the disappointment of doctors and bonesetters	118
Last days for a train of thought	121
Wembley '66	124
Mikey ahead of his time	127
The day 'The Yank' had the last laugh	130
Crack 100 in the Dusk	133
Cheltenham Pilgrimage	136
Nissaning to spoken music	139
Exploring the hidden Lancashire	142
On your bike	144
The Glory days return for Kerry	148
Michael Rides To Glory	150
An age of innocence and hope	153
Foreword to Brendan Fullam's book	156
Ladies reach untold heights	159
Requiem for a sad hero	162
The Cockney Boy	165
A great newspaper man	167

FOREWORD

SOMETHING extraordinary happened the art of sportswriting in 1973. A wandering McGillycuddy Reek arrived from Kerry to raise the craft to new heights.

His revolution was as simple as it was devastating. Sportswriters had long learned to augment the staple diet of statistics and times and scores with colour, analysis, and observations from the participants.

The writing of Con Houlihan rejuvenated a profession under threat from broadcast media The copy he produced for the back page of the Evening Press in such volume for so long (four evenings a week), and produces now for the Sunday World, defies categorisation.

The clipped style, the short paragraphs, the wordplay, give the game away: here is a man driven by a love of poetry as much as a love of sport.

Not for Con the norms of the profession: the eloquently overstated descriptions of mundane events, the invocation of martial terminology, the attribution of cliched and meaningless quotes to "hundred and ten per cent" footballers.

Con's perspective is that of the supporter. Long before fanzines and sentimental football fiction became fashionable, Con conveyed the sense of belonging of the fans. He writes unapologetically as a lover of sport, prepared to suffer wind and snow on the off-chance of seeing something magnificent on a racecourse or sportsfield.

When he can, Con sacrifices even the press box perspective of great games to climb the terrace and stand alongside the *cosmhuintir* of the great occasions he covers. This is territory he has made his own, a bottomless well of sporting lore.

This meant that Con's perspective on events was often from the cheapest spot in the house. Although occasionally banished to the press section in Lansdowne Road or in events far from home, he could be found on the same spot at the Canal End in Croke Park week after week. One of the Dublin players describes his only attempt at a shot as being so wayward that "I almost hit Con Houlihan."

He became the fan's columnist.

Perhaps because he is one.

To those of us who came of age in his company, that back page was to become part of the experience of the sporting event itself. The final whistle might have sounded, the winner all right declared, but the atmosphere lingered until Con had been read.

There was always something special in Con's account, a surprise that nobody else in an attendance of sixty or seventy thousand could possibly have perceived.

His perspective on great events is always different from everyone else's. His description of Mike Sheehy's goal against Paddy Cullen in the 1978 All Ireland final, which described Cullen returning to the goalmouth "like a woman who smelled a cake burning" and his comment that Seamus Darby was "the wren who stowed away on the eagle's plumage" are the definitive descriptions of the two most famous goals in GAA history.

As Con never ceases to remind us, he comes from Kerry, the county of Maurice Walsh, of Brendan Kennelly, of John B Keane, of Sigerson Clifford.

That put him three points up before the throw-in, able to draw on the natural poetry of the landscape in which he grew up, where even the placenames are full of song: Knocknagoshel, Gneeveguilla, Lyrecrompane.

Herein we will find a reference to what must be proudest by-line of all: "From Con Houlihan in Knocknagoshel" (on an account of a soccer match from Paris, but *sin sceal eile*).

His references to the culture of an impoverished but incredibly literate age in the Irish countryside, Kickham, Carbery, Ireland's Own and Roddy the Rover, fitted surprisingly easily into the format of a brash Dublin evening newspaper.

As Kerry is next door to America, (if only spiritually since the continental plates so carelessly drifted apart), Con lined his verbal armoury with American literary influences, as well was the sportswriting canon of Ring Lardner, Jim Murray, Grantland Rice and Red Smith.

And he turned it all into something that Irish journalism had never seen before.

This selection of pieces from the dying days of the Irish Press group and the Sunday World will project the reader backwards to the 1970s and 1980s, and, in a strange way, forwards too.

No other writer has carried such clarity in their love of sport, from the wet hedge where teams togged out a generation or two ago in Lyrecrompane or Gneeveguilla, to the corporate hospitality quarters of an all seater stadiums.

This clarity of vision sits equally easily in an era when followers of sport are becoming, as Con so eloquently puts it, "watchers of Sky, as distinct from astronomers and astrologers."

He takes that clarity of vision to bigger sporting issues.

On the supporters of Glasgow's two soccer clubs, Celtic and Rangers, he wrote in 1989: "football isn't part of their culture - it is more or less their only culture." The description dwarfs anything else you will find in the volumes of books, acres of newsprint, and entire sociological industry devoted to that city's soccertarian divide.

Over the years the followers of the back page were gently introduced to a few secrets. An otherworld was woven of life in the mountains around Castleisland, and its mythological Latin quarter.

In this collection, some revisionism has crept in. Con attempts to convince us that "tea in the bog is no different from tea elsewhere, if someone likes it strong, he waits until it has been allowed to draw beyond the average."

In an unguarded moment, he reveals the key to the success of Con's Back Page, when he tells us "Of course I miss the bog and of course I miss the fishing," he says, "and believe me, I am not overprone to nostalgia."

Fans, particularly those who have grown up in an Ireland coming to terms with its sense of place in both the material and sporting worlds, know what it is to miss something without feeling nostalgic for it,

By banishing sentiment from his accounts of tea from a bottle in the bog or of Herculean feats of sporting heroes gone by, Con elevated those enticing, short-paragraphed Back Page columns to an art form in itself.

It was on the Back Page of the Evening Press that he lived and breathed, a companion to all of us when Ireland came of age in a sporting sense, learning to compete and win once more in the sporting world.

Con is no longer on the back page, but plies his trade in the colourful, fast-moving culture of the Sunday World, comfortable among a new generation of fans.

Con helps us see it in all its colourful best. He makes great sporting occasions greater. He has shown us all what sportswriting can be.

EOGHAN CORRY

INTRODUCTION

I am not too sure about my reasons for publishing this collection; it is hardly for fame and certainly not for fortune.

I suspect that essentially it is an attempt to salvage something from the loss of our own little Titanic, the good ship Evening Press.

The articles appear here almost exactly as they did originally - and if you find mystifying references to "yesterday" or "last week", bear with me – editing might diminish spontaneity.

There is a certain sadness attached to this little book: it resides in the headlines; almost all were composed by Shane Flynn or myself or by both of us.

Shane has departed this mortal world. We were friends and colleagues for almost a quarter of a century.

Shane had a consummate knowledge of what went into making The Evening Press and indeed The Irish Press and The Sunday Press – he often made me feel like an outsider.

I had one up on him: there were times after football games on the Continent when I was in Burgh Quay at about three o'clock or some such ungodly hour – then only the security man at the back door and myself were in that vast building.

Shane, for better or worse, never had that experience; if he envied me, it was a mark of our camaraderie – it was all great fun.

All the articles are from The Evening Press, unless otherwise stated. I hope that you will enjoy The Back Page.

Monday, August 28, 1989

Mo and the jungle

A little before seven o'clock last Saturday evening an orange-haired fresh-faced young man of medium height and neat build, flanked by two tall and burly men, entered the check-in area at Glasgow airport; a casual observer might have thought that he was seeing someone being discreetly taken to prison – in fact, the young man in the middle was a professional footballer in danger of his life.

If you said that to our imaginary casual observer, it would take you a very long time to explain to him why a decent law-abiding man should have thousands of otherwise normal people willing him grievous bodily harm – or worse.

About three months ago Maurice Johnston was idolised by those same people; it seemed certain that he was on his way back to Glasgow Celtic after a spell campaigning in France; then in an astonishing turn-around he signed for Glasgow Rangers; the fatted calf was spared – the prodigal son went into hiding.

Money plays a big part in the lives of professional footballers; in Johnston's case it seems to play an inordinate part; his senior career spans only nine years – but Rangers are his fifth club.

Last July he signed for the highest bidder; Rangers, backed by powerful business corporations, are among the richest clubs in the world.

And this to Celtic's swarm of devotees seemed an act of treachery that put him in the same bracket as Judas and Lord Haw-Haw and George Blake.

How could you go about explaining this to our imaginary casual observer? You would need to go back a long way, back even to the generation before The Great Famine – already the Irish were flocking across the narrow seas to the burgeoning cities of industrial Britain.

London, Birmingham, Manchester, and Liverpool were the promised lands for the Irish from most parts of the island; Glasgow and Edinburgh were the new worlds for the people of the North-West.

And in Glasgow especially the influx added an element of tribal warfare to a city long inured to violence.

In Merseyside the religious aspect has long since diminished into insignificance: the rivalry between Liverpool and Everton is fierce and unremitting but edged with respect. Glasgow is a different kettle of people: the old city by the Clyde is a living paradox; it has long had a great reputation for engineering and scholarship – and violence.

One of its more famous sons, the nineteenth-century poet James Thomson, christened it 'The City of Dreadful Night'.

It was already a fertile breeding-ground for hatred before the immigrant Irish were accused of bringing disease and creating unemployment by working for a pittance.

The hatred became formalised when soccer evolved; the foundation of Celtic in 1888 gave the immigrants and the descendants of immigrants a flagship.

Unless you have been to a clash between Celtic and Rangers, you can hardly begin to understand the raw hostility that rages between the devotees of these clubs.

Essentially it springs from frustration: for generations the nucleus of both armies has been drawn from low down on the economic ladder, from people who lived as best they could in hovels and tenements; now the housing is improved – but the new corporation and council estates are bleak, soulless places.

For many football isn't just part of their culture – it is more or less their only culture: their dreams and hopes are compressed into a few hours on Saturday afternoons.

And they do not look on themselves as followers or supporters; they would deem such words effete; those who sport the royal blue and the green-and-white are participants, back-up soldiers whose tumultuous zeal is vital to the cause of the troops at the front.

Whether they meet at Parkhead or Ibrox or Hampden Park, the atmosphere is thunderous; it gives you an inkling of the mental climate that washed around the scaffold when execution was a public spectacle – but with the difference that only the match can tell who is the executioner and who is the victim.

A meeting of Celtic and Rangers is never an ordinary occasion; the Johnston factor made Saturday unique; his was almost the only Rangers' name in the pub conversation before the match; the few Celtic names mentioned were of the men who were deemed most eager to clobber him.

He would be done – I was repeatedly assured of that. And it would happen off the ball. The name of the most likely hitman was not, seemingly, a secret.

The morning was cold and showery; the rain cleared away but the sky remained grey and cloudy; at Parkhead the lights came on at two o'clock.

And already the Red Cross people were wheeling away men and boys for whom the occasion had proved too much. There were less girls and women than usual – and hardly any children; Hillsborough is casting a long shadow.

In The Albany Bar I had heard sensible people speculating on the possibility of a riot if Johnston got clobbered or if he dared to score a goal.

To our casual observer it might seem alcohol-induced fantasy; it wasn't – I knew all too well what a senior executive meant when he said: "Mo doesn't understand the mood of The Jungle..."

The Jungle is the terrace at the London Road end – it is Celtic's sacred place. On Saturday it was ominously quiet in the hour before tip-off time.

Normally you would hear renderings of 'The Boys From The County Armagh' and see the tricolours waving like a mad forest.

There was a terrible and terrifying seriousness about Saturday; the police were present in strength but you felt that they would need back-up from the army if the torrent of hatred burst its banks.

The minutes seemed to crawl as they approached three o'clock; at last the ball-boys came out from the tunnel under The East Stand; for a few seconds the partisans seemed to hold their breath.

And then as the teams emerged, the eruption was such that it might have caused the clouds to spill their rain.

The vocal storm was accompanied by thunder-like drumming on the wood of the stands. The fusion was soul stunning.

And then came the announcing of the team sheets; the name of Rangers' number ten brought a synchronised howl of execration – I was near enough to see Mo Johnston's face go white.

It was a blessed relief when play began.

Wednesday, August 30, 1989

Ray Wilkins, seventeen years later

Ray Wilkins was captain of Chelsea before he could vote; if ever there was a Golden Boy, it was he; this is his seventeenth season as a senior professional; he has earned a great deal of money and captained England – and yet the general feeling is that he has failed to fulfill his promise.

A lot of ale and wine and spirits has gone down the red lane since first I watched him play; it was on that night at Wembley when a lad named David O'Leary played with an assurance that belied his tender years.

That game against England ended 1-1; we celebrated as if we had brought off a famous victory; I didn't bother about bed; I had to have about twelve hundred words of deathless prose ready for this paper by eight o'clock.

It was my first foreign assignment, only that of course I didn't look on England as foreign. And that morning as I walked down to Fleet Street from a hotel in Piccadilly, I was as happy as a rabbit in a patch of lettuce.

It had been an exceedingly dry summer; the grass in Hyde Park was brown and the leaves were withered; as we went down to the Tube station after the match, the first drops of rain for several weeks began to fall.

I was with David Faiers, God rest him – he knew the underground system as well as Mark Twain knew the Mississippi.

There was a big element of West Indians on the train; in the previous week there had been trouble at the Notting Hill carnival – they had come to Wembley to show their solidarity with another minority.

My other memories of that occasion long ago include the journey from Heathrow into London on the evening before the match.

On the coach I met Billy George* and discovered to my astonishment that it was his first time journeying to England's capital.

And as I named the places by which we passed and pointed out such landmarks as Brentford's Stadium and Hammersmith Bridge and Fuller's brewery, I felt like Marco Polo bringing a tiro with him on a return visit to Cathay.

It was innocence, dear reader – sheer crazy innocence.

Billy had arranged to meet a colleague in an establishment called The Kings and Keys; thus I became acquainted with Andy Byrne, then the governor of that homely little pub.

He recognised me from the Evening Press; I was delighted – it was friendship at first sight.

Next morning I acquired another friend; his first words to me were more than somewhat perceptive – "You look as if you could do with a cup of tea."

Thus spoke Jack Craddock whose magic fingers performed on the telex in The Irish Press office across the street from The Kings and Keys.

That morning the bould Jack suffered his first experience of my handwriting; to get over the shock he brewed another pot of tea.

Jack is back in Burgh Quay now after a long spell in London – and he retains his infallible instinct for sensing when I am in need of a cup of tea.

He is a Dub, bred and born and reared; I suspect, however, that he misses London – to some degree; outside of Ireland it is my favourite place; Jack, I know, feels that way too.

How do I know? Many's the time I heard him finding fault with the city and its denizens – but it was obviously a lovers' quarrel; Jack's knowledge of London was so intimate that it gave the game away.

Alas, the Fleet Street that we loved is no more: the Daily Mail is the last national paper to be printed there; soon it too departs – and Carmelite House will become another hive of yuppies.

When last I was in The Kings and Keys, I didn't recognise a soul or even a body on either side of the counter.

And the scent of beer and metal and ink had been replaced by the stink of aftershave lotion.

All these memories tumbled back to me about five minutes to three in Glasgow last Saturday when Ray Wilkins trotted out onto the pitch at Parkhead in the blue shirt of Rangers.

And I remembered too what I had written about him a very long time ago – that he was the epitome of what modern coaching has produced.

Technically he is as close to perfection as a human can be; about his dedication there has never been any doubt; you will search in vain for his name in the front pages – and yet Ray lacks the element that would enable him to cross the river into greatness.

His fieldmark is the long cross-pitch pass; he got little chance to employ it on Saturday.

Indeed he got little chance to make any kind of decent pass atall; it was an occasion when the play was so frenzied that to 'dwell' on the ball was as easy as thatching a roof in a storm.

And Wilkins resembled a gourmet who had been invited to a banquet which turned out to be an eating contest.

For most of the first half he looked not so much bewitched as bothered and bewildered; the texture of the play and the pace of his counterpart, Paul McStay, caused him to resemble a terrier being teased by a greyhound.

His frustration caused him to perpetrate a most uncharacteristic deed; late in the first half as he went down in a tangle with Peter Grant, he put a boot into the back of the Celt's knee.

I hadn't been so astounded since Alan Dukes cast doubts on the parentage of a certain senior clergyman.

And so we witnessed Ray Wilkins being shown the yellow card; it was a moment that bordered on unreality, almost as if Pan Collins had charged Gay Byrne with being unprofessional.

Fair dues to the little man, he stuck to his task – and acting no doubt on the principle about how you should comport yourself in Rome, he interpreted the even-chance ball as liberally as the rest of the cast.

Mr. Syme produced the yellow card six times in all – and yet it was far from being a violent or unsporting match.

Indeed the pitch resembled an oasis of sanity in a world that had gone temporarily insane.

On a few occasions I saw a player helping up a recumbent opponent; good professionals respect one another.

So indeed should good amateurs as the hurling men of Offaly hinted when they made their historic gesture after their match against Antrim.

And you can say what you like about Maurice Johnston – and thousands are saying it – but you cannot deny his courage.

How it will all work out I do not know but I suspect that after Saturday he has got the worst behind him.

And yet I feel that Mo will need his bodyguard for quite a while yet; there is always the danger of some fanatic setting out to become a folk hero.

On Saturday evening the mood outside Parkhead was obscene; taxis were as rare on London Road as donkey-carts in Piccadilly.

*Doyen of The Cork Examiner.

Friday, April 16, 1993

A great writer in Croke Park

I have written elsewhere about Robert Lynd, the great journalist, whose life seemed a putting of flesh on the philosophy of Wolfe Tone.

Once when consigned to a hospital conducted by Catholic nuns, he was asked his religion – and declared himself a Presbyterian, kind of; it was a fair enough description of one who was marvellously free from prejudice, probably because he grew up in Belfast.

Lynd was a great lover of many games and an aficionado of several; rugby seems to have been his favourite; hurling might have superseded it if he had known more about it.

He was in his fifties when he witnessed his first sample of the ancient game; he was in Dublin to write a piece about an early edition of The Hospitals' Sweepstakes – and made the pilgrimage to Croke Park.

He might not have been in Dublin atall but for a bitter debate on sweepstakes that had erupted in The House Of Parliament; he was dispatched to see at first hand this demonic lottery that was causing such emotional distress in Britain.

On the way he pondered whether it is more demoralising to win £30,000 or to lose ten shillings and decided that it is better to have loved money and lost than never to have loved money atall.

As soon as he was settled in Dublin, he took a walk in Stephen's Green; "Birds were singing above children at play and the world was in flower in the still evening."

The next day was The Sabbath; that didn't inhibit the Presbyterian (kind of) from going to Croke Park to watch a joust between Dublin and Limerick.

"How charming the teams looked in the brilliant green of Limerick and the brilliant blue of Dublin!"

And, of course, there was a band – "pipers… dressed in green kilts and with flowing saffron robes, many wearing feathers in their caps."

The players walked two by two, "a green-shirted man beside a blue-shirted man, each carrying a hurley, the weapon used in the game."

The use of the word 'weapon' is interesting; Lynd seemingly saw the game as a substitute for battle – which to some degree it is.

The use of the word 'shirt' is also interesting; it isn't long since a

Catholic priest in this country objected to that word in the context of Gaelic games.

Seemingly it smacked too much of soccer. How culturally exclusive can we be...

Anyhow, whether 'shirt' or 'jersey' was the more appropriate, the game went on – and both alarmed and enthralled our visitor.

It didn't start, of course, without a building up of a head of steam; the pipers rendered 'ancient, warlike airs,' including The Bold Fenian Men. Times haven't changed much.

Lynd goes on to say: "One could not help regretting that no Irish painter has ever arisen to perpetuate on canvas the colours of the hurling field as Degas perpetuated the colours of the racecourse and the ballet."

I second his lament; most of our painters, alas, look on sport as unworthy of their art.

The game begins. Lynd writes: "I do not know the rules of hurling but, as a moral equivalent to war, it seems to me to be about the only rival of Rugby football."

He goes on: "It is said to be the original form of hockey; some people have described it as hockey without rules.'

I know of a Cockney who calls it "a kind of wild 'ockey."

Let us listen to Lynd: "Hurleys... rise into the air like weapons of war and the player is allowed to do almost anything he likes with his hurley except deliberately hit a player on the other side."

Of course Lynd was apprehensive; almost everyone watching his first game of hurling cannot but be.

"Hurleys meet in the air with a wild crashing of wood; one of them is broken into two pieces, and small boys rush into the field in a struggle to retrieve a broken blade as a memento.

"The casualties to sticks certainly went into the double figures. The casualties to players were less numerous... but the ambulance men must have been on the field about eight times."

Robert Lynd couldn't help feeling glad that there was no international hurling.

"Imagine a game ... played between France and Scotland." Indeed.... the soul boggles.

The truth, of course, is that when hurling is well played and well refereed, it is a far less dangerous game than Rugby.

Lynd goes on: "It is certainly a swift and beautiful game, calling into play all the skills of eye and hand and foot."

He says that it is worth crossing The Irish Sea to see a man catching the ball amidst a frenzy of hurley-wielding opponents and sending it up the field into the goalmouth.

It is a pity that he didn't live to see Tony Doran plucking the ball from a forest of ash and palming it over the bar or into the net.

Lynd doesn't tell us who won the game but I suspect that it was the men in brilliant green.

"On the whole the Limerick men seemed to be about a quarter of a second faster than the Dublin men in everything they did and it looked at half-time as if they would run through them..."

It didn't prove to be as simple as he foresaw; Dublin had a man who was inspired and inspiring.

'There was... a Dublin back who played like a demi-god and who was always a quarter of a second faster than any Limerick man who was near him.'

He goes on: "Even when a game is one-sided, an invincible player can keep it exciting to the end."

As Lynd walks away from Croke Park, a friend says: "After this, I don't think you need feel nervous about going to a bullfight."

———

Friday, May 7, 1993

Recalling glory at Goodison...

It was the 21st of September in 1949; I was then studying about fourteen hours a day – this didn't prevent The Republic of Ireland* from achieving a sensational victory over England in Goodison Park in the heart of Liverpool.

I didn't even watch that game on the wireless. Was it broadcast at all?

In the context of our recent game with Denmark, we in the Evening Press issued a little quiz about soccer; one answer was wrong – I take complete responsibility.

The question asked you to name the only League of Ireland player on that famous team; I was convinced the Tommy O'Connor had that honour.

I have got several letters and a few phone calls pointing out my own goal; seemingly our keeper, Tommy Godwin, was still playing on the auld sod.

There is a lovely ending to that great story: the two local heroes came back on the Mail Boat that night and found a little party of aficionados waiting to acclaim them.

They were chaired some distance along the pier and then allowed to go off to their breakfast.

You will often hear pub discussions about that amazing game – and almost inevitably someone will ask you to name the immortal eleven.

So now for once and for all I will write it down – in the formation that prevailed at the time.

                    Tommy Godwin
Jackie Carey   Bud Aherne
                    Con Martin
Willie Walsh   Tommy Moroney
    Peter Desmond   Peter Farrell
Peter Corr   Tommy O'Connor
                    Davey Walsh

Young people may be somewhat puzzled by the formation which I have outlined – I will do my best to explain.

In those days the term "back four" was unknown; there were two full-backs and a centre-back.

The two wing-halves were basically midfielders whose first duty was in defence. The two in front of them were midfielders whose first duty was in attack. They were called inside-forwards.

There were three men up front – two wingers and a centre-forward.

Of course in practice this formation wasn't as rigid as it looked on paper but, all in all, backs were backs and forwards were forwards.

That game in Goodison Park was a friendly; it drew a remarkable crowd – over 51,000 paid in.

It is part of folklore that a celebrated journalist, Henry Rose of the Daily Express, wrote that he would eat his hat if the visitors won.

Folklore doesn't tell us whether he kept his promise.

Godwin was the especial hero of that autumn day long ago; he seemed magnetic.

Con Martin scored from a penalty after half-an-hour; I seem to remember that Bert Williams got a good touch – but the ball spun just over the line.

England mounted a long siege in the second half; Peter Farrell put the issue beyond doubt when he scored in a breakaway six minutes from full time.

Who managed our expedition on that mission impossible? Was there any manager?

I know that Tom Scully was the chairman of the selectors; perhaps he was the manager too.

It is more likely that Jackie Carey, the captain, was the acting manager.

I suspect that it was Carey who was responsible for my involvement with Manchester United.

He began his senior career with St. James's Gate, then a great power in the land.

United paid £250 for him; it was a small sum even by the standard of the time.

You can work it out for yourself by comparing the wages of that era to the wages of today.

I will hazard a guess; the average industrial wage then was about three pounds a week; the fee paid for Jackie was about eighty weeks' wages.

And so in a rough-and-ready way you could say that £250 in 1936 would correspond to about £15,000 today.

The comparison isn't very realistic because in that sensible age transfer fees were in real money – now they are often only figures on paper.

The war carved a huge gap in Carey's career; he became a folk hero at Old Trafford – and captained United when they won the FA Cup in 1948.

He was still captain when they won the League title in 1952.

He captained The Rest Of The World against Great Britain in 1947.

He went into management but didn't last very long; as far as I know, he ended his working career with the local council in Blackburn.

Some of that team became well known to me, especially Con Martin and Peter Farrell and Tommy O'Connor – it was a privilege.

I knew Tommy Moroney since my student days in Cork's fair city.

He was then campaigning with the great club that fought out of The Mardyke.

He was a brilliant out-half in his school days and if he hadn't gone over to soccer, he might have played for Ireland.

There was a great bond between Cork and West Ham in those days; Tommy was one of many who went from the banks to Upton Park.

There was a woeful dearth of butter for several years after the war – and this led to a rather strange link between myself and West Ham.

Our family were involved in the creamery business and I was able to send over the odd few pounds of butter on the old Inisfallen.

It was collected at Paddington and greatly appreciated.

It was illegal to send butter out of the country then but I doubt if the gardai will come knocking at my door now.

I managed to smuggle it over because I knew some of the lads on the Inisfallen.

And in the context of that smuggled butter I can claim to have played a tiny part in that famous victory in Goodison Park on the 21st of September in 1949

* Should it be Eire?

Thursday, June 1, 1989

Downfall of a hero

Here in Manchester in the small hours of the morning it was wet and cold; the foyer of the Portland Hotel resembled a wakehouse as a crowd of Barry McGuigan's supporters, many in evening dress, bemoaned the downfall of their hero.

Shock mingled with sadness. And over all hung an air of anti-climax, not so much because the fight had ended so abruptly but because the former World Champion had looked so unlike his old self.

In the record books this fight will be labelled r.s.f. – cut eye – but any of Barry's admirers who believe that otherwise he might have won are deceiving themselves.

The truth is that he was in trouble long before the referee, Mickey Vann, decided that the cut was too deep to allow the fight to continue; Barry's seconds protested but it was only a gesture. And afterwards the former champion said that he was fit to go on but I believe that Mr. Vann did him a great favour.

It was a disconcerting occasion for Barry and his camp; if Jim McDonnell had been picked as a soft touch, someone blundered. He was far from being a lamb for the sacrifice – indeed he was more like the tiger to which Barry is often compared.

In the popular scenario the Irish Cockney would depend on his greater speed of foot and hope to win on points but it didn't work out that way.

It was quickly obvious that McDonnell was prepared to stand and fight; his plan of campaign was clear – he went all out to deny McGuigan his accustomed dominance of the ring's centre.

And as the fight didn't go according to plan, you could sense a growing bewilderment in McGuigan and his corner.

It was hard to believe that we were watching the same man who by sheer strength and aggression wore down Julio Miranda in eight rounds at Pickett's Lock last December.

And the submerged truth surfaced again last night – despite his great fusion of courage and strength, Barry is amazingly vulnerable under fire. This was seen in the seventh round of his fight with Danilo Cabrera in Ballsbridge and again in the fifth round of his fight with Miranda.

And it was seen most clearly of all that night in Las Vegas; Barry was clearly ahead after five rounds but suddenly was hit by a flurry in the sixth and almost crumbled before Steve Cruz.

Last night he began with his usual aggression; indeed at the bell he pushed the referee aside – but McDonnell refused to be overawed and at no time did he step back more than two or three paces.

McGuigan perhaps won the first round. He was the more aggressive – McDonnell was cautioned for holding and punching. Nevertheless, it was clear that Barry's corner was far from happy in the minute's break. And his huge following who afforded the accustomed adulation as he came into the ring were strangely quiet.

Barry perhaps won the second round too. Again McDonnell was warned for holding and hitting – and midway through the round he buckled under a fierce body blow. His followers, however, were becoming increasingly vociferous and at the bell they chanted "Here We Go, Here We Go". It was a strange reversal.

McDonnell's following numbered about 300 in a crowd of over 8,000 – the rest were clearly in favour of the Monaghan man.

Round Three began with the usual McGuigan flourish; this time it was edged with desperation because blood was seeping from a cut on the right eyebrow. And you felt that Barry knew that unless he finished the fight soon, he would have to retire.

He never looked like landing a telling blow; this was clearly McDonnell's round. In the second minute he landed a looping left; McGuigan's knees buckled and he almost went down. His followers were silent – and the other crowd were on their feet. Barry was glad to hear the bell.

Obviously his corner men did a good job on his eye because at the start of the round the blood seemed to have been stopped but he made no attempt to guard the cut – and McDonnell's favourite punch, a looping left, got through time and again.

About midway through the round the blood began to flow; Mr. Vann took a long look – and it was obvious that all was over.

McDonnell's following surged from their area and surrounded the ring but all was in good order; that was typical of this highly-organised occasion.

Wednesday, June 14, 1989

Bull's eye of the turf.

Sometimes someone comes along who points out truths that are obvious to him or her but not to the generality; in a generation or so those truths are apparent to everybody – and then that person is labelled a genius.

Such a one was Phil Bull who departed his mortal world a few days ago.

Only two people can be deemed great reformers in British racing – and inevitably far beyond; they could hardly have differed more in their backgrounds.

Henry John Rous was an admiral and a Conservative M.P.; Phil Bull was the son of a coal miner and an unremitting adversary of the Establishment.

Rous was known as The Dictator of the Turf; he saved racing at a time

– about the middle of the last century – when it was in danger of death from its own degeneracy; he is best remembered, however, as the man who devised the weight-for-age format.

Bull was an expert on breeding and a brilliant judge of horses, especially on the flat; he advocated starting stalls long before the idea took root in Britain; he was best known, however, as the publisher of Timeform.

I knew him well by sight in later years; he was a low-sized sturdy man but with his spectacularly long white beard he stood out at the race-track.

Outsize spectacles and the ever-present cigar reinforced the image of individuality, if not of eccentricity.

Such outward shows were irrelevant; what marked out Phil Bull was the wonderful lucidity of his mind.

It was often said that he wasted himself by his devotion to racing – that he would have been a towering success in the world of politics or finance; to some extent he agreed – he called the sport of kings a great triviality.

And yet it is unlikely that he regretted his choice: he had no patience for committees and hence would hardly have been an effective politician – and financial wizards tend to take more out of the common pool than they put into it.

Bull gave a multitude of people a great deal of pleasure – there are worse epitaphs.

He was born in the South Yorkshire coalfield eighty years ago; the location probably influenced him towards his vocation – within striking distance were Pontefract, Doncaster, Wetherby, Ripon, Thirsk, York, Beverley and Market Rasen.

His family background probably helped too: miners have a special bond with horses; they worked with them in the old days and the racehorse represented an image of freedom and brightness for men who spent so much of their lives in dark confines.

Many famous jockeys have been miners' sons: Gordon and Cliff Richards are examples; so are Manny and Joe Mercer – of course their small physique pointed them toward the profession but there was probably more to it than that.

Phil Bull made his racing debut at Pontefract; he was all of nine and accompanied by a sister who was a year less.

Miners weren't too well paid seventy years ago; young Phil decided to keep his few shillings for a punt or two.

I have heard him tell the story on television: he went in his Sunday suit complete with the white rose of Yorkshire in his buttonhole, presented himself at the members' enclosure and told the gateman that he bore a message for his grandfather.

He named this imagined ancestor as a noble lord; he and the wee lass were ushered in and had a most enjoyable day.

And young Phil came home convinced of two things – that in some way he would eventually make his living out of the turf and that he was every bit as good as his supposed betters.

Nine was a rather tender age for setting up as a bookmaker or starting out as a gambler; young Bull continued on at school; eventually he graduated with a B.Sc. in Mathematics.

I have no doubt that he was a good teacher but that didn't cause him to lose sight of what he believed was his destiny.

And even good teachers are like good mariners; they look to the day when they can take a shore job.

Phil Bull tip-toed towards his destiny; he began by publishing a little pamphlet which was the fore-runner of Timeform.

The seed fell on fertile ground and grew; he wasn't, as has been claimed, the first to make punters aware of how important time is in assessing a horse's chances – but he disseminated the idea.

And he prospered, so much so that by thirty he was able to leave the classroom behind him; chalk and blackboard would still play a big part in his life – but mostly under the open sky.

Phil Bull put his money where his mathematical calculations were; he became one of the boldest and most successful punters in modern British racing.

Alex Bird is the only one usually named in the same bracket – and Barney Curley is working at it.

Phil Bull's first onslaught on racing's establishment horrified The Jockey Club; he maintained that The Rules of Racing inordinately favoured speedy two-year-olds at the expense of two-year-olds bred to stay.

At the time two-year-olds were not allowed to run over seven furlongs before September 1; Bull's persistence got the date brought forward to July 1.

He went further; in 1961 he persuaded the authorities to allow him sponsor a mile race for two-year-olds – thus was born the Timeform Gold Cup.

Long before that inaugural running at Doncaster, the teacher turned guru and punter had become an owner.

His first outstanding horse was Orgoglio, winner of The Champagne Stakes and The Victoria Cup.

In 1956 his Arisetta finished third in the One Thousand Guineas – that was his nearest shot at a classic.

In 1957 he finished fifth in the owners' list – with 18 races worth a total of £26,000. It sounds like unsalted peanuts now – but inflation and sponsorship have vastly transformed the scene.

Phil Bull is said to have made his 'foundation' money on the great northern colt, Dante.

As a two-year-old he was a sensation – and Bull was on him from the start.

Younger readers may be surprised to learn that the classics went on during the 1939-'45 war – they did but at Newmarket; Epsom was army territory.

And in the spring of 1948 Dante was looked on as a certainty for The Guineas; Court Martial headed him – and Bull was said to have lost all he had won on the runner-up as a two-year-old.

Dante recompensed him in The Derby; the son of Nearco and Rosy Legend won a famous victory – I am prejudiced; I backed him.

Phil Bull's legacy didn't end with Timeform and the reformation of the two-year-old scene; he more than most was responsible for the introduction of starting stalls and overnight declarations.

All in all, it was an immense achievement for one born into a family with no racing background.

Admiral Rous, after all, was taking on members of his own class; a century later a coal miner's son brought about reforms equally sweeping.

And aspects of racing which we now take for granted owe their origin to two men who had little in common except lucid minds and stubborn wills.

There was also, of course, their passionate love of racing; Phil Bull called it a triviality – but he put in the word 'great'.

Friday, June 23, 1989

From the screen to the green

Philip Walton experienced the kind of finish yesterday evening that caused him to eat a hearty supper.

On the eighteenth green at sun-blessed Portmarnock he faced up to a 21-yard free – with the difference that the target was rather smaller than that in hurling or Gaelic football.

With the absence of fuss that is the coursemark of his game he stroked the ball boldly; it was clear that he had the length – the accuracy was in question.

About three feet from the hole the little white sphere veered slightly to the right but quickly changed its mind.

Then a foot from the hole it wobbled left and then right – and then as if drawn by a magnet, it trickled into the cup.

And I suspect that the applause carried down as far as Balgriffin.

Philip is a local lad – from Malahide or thereabouts – and he certainly didn't lack for support yesterday.

Irish golf crowds are famous for their sportsmanship; they applaud good deeds no matter what their source – but they are human and therefore inclined towards tribalism.

There was a palpable example yesterday afternoon; it occurred on the eleventh green.

Mark McNulty, one of Walton's two partners, sank a twenty-footer and was warmly applauded; Walton got down from ten feet and ecstasy erupted.

Some optimist shouted "Here we go" and at the next hole it seemed that he could be right.

The twelfth at Ireland's most celebrated links is only 149 yards – but that statistic masks its wicked nature.

Two evil humps guard the green; they are aided and abetted by a pair of steep bunkers.

If your tee shot doesn't land on the green, your round could be devastated.

Walton drove first – with a weapon that resembled a nine iron; the ball came to rest about eight feet to the left of the pin; great was the applause.

McNulty drove next; the ball ended up about twelve feet to the right of the flag; he was warmly applauded. The third partner, Jose Maria Olazabal, put his ball halfway between McNulty's and the pin. The crowd gave him his due – this was sweet golf.

Walton got his birdie – and the aforementioned optimist shouted "On your way."

I might as well tell you that the young Spaniard was also down in two; McNulty got a par.

The friendly Zimbabwean is no stranger to Ireland; three years ago he tied for second place in this tournament.

Olazabal too has good memories of this country; he was joint runner-up in The Open last year.

Philip finished yesterday in 68; Jose Maria returned a 69; Mark is still a contender with 71.

I followed this trio for an obvious reason; I am as much a chauvinist as the Australian Prime Minister, whatever his name is.

Philip Walton, fair-haired and white-visored, stood out yesterday; it is easy to understand his popularity – he is at once simple and stylish.

I am not forgetting Ronan Rafferty; he went around in 67 – but he was in the clubhouse or thereabouts before I reached the course, hard by the village which the locals call The Marnick.

He was only three shots behind Sandy Lyle – but most of the talk on the course and in the bars centred on the Scot.

And an aficionado who had followed his every stroke said to me: "Sam Torrance was inside him at every hole – and yet Lyle finished seven strokes in front of him."

And he went on: "And after his lunch he practised for two hours". How he found out this, I don't know – and it would have been impolite to ask.

Sandy Lyle occupies a strange niche in the mythology of golf – strange even for a Scot.

For long years he was the Golden Boy who was threatening to make 'potential' an extremely dirty word.

He reached his nadir one rain-drenched evening when he tore up his card a few holes from the finish in The Irish Open – at Royal Dublin, I think.

And then over a few glorious days it all came right: the English-reared Scot won The British Open.

Financially that victory set him up for life – but seemingly despite all the Scotsman jokes, he is not materially minded.

His life's ambition is to play good golf – something he hasn't been doing for a long time.

Until yesterday he most certainly wasn't having a season in the sun.

He had invoked several coaches, including his father – all in vain.

Obviously he hasn't heard of Sean Boylan; instead of consulting Ireland's most famous witch-doctor, he called in a psychiatrist – worse still, a fellow Scot.

Nevertheless, it all changed yesterday – and our Sandy tore up not his card but the course record.

Before setting out for the daunting North County, I watched the play on television – and saw as much as I could.

Lyle's driving was steady rather than spectacular; he created that marvellous 64 by some super play on the green.

He sank big putts at the 3rd, 10th, 13th and 17th – and a huge putt at the 12th, as long as Walton's at the 18th.

Sandy is immensely popular with Irish crowds, probably because his human frailty makes us feel kinship with him.

I am not forgetting my neighbours' child, Eoghan O'Connell, the amateur (for the time being) who came home in 68.

Some people think that a Kerry golfer is a kind of freak – far from it.

Eoghan is following in a line that contains Billy O'Sullivan, John Guerin, Pat Mulcaire, John C. Cooper – and Bridget Gleeson.

John C., an old friend of mine, had tremendous talent at Gaelic football, rugby, and golf.

He was, however, always too busy making a living; running a hotel consumes enormous skelps of time.

About him there is a story which could be deemed a Kerryman joke but is absolutely true.

It concerns a day long ago when he had to come up to Dublin to buy a few knives from Broderick's down the quay.

It happened to be the first day of The Irish Open – and John C. had put his name down just for the heaven of it.

He cruised around Woodbrook (I think) in 66 – and found himself at the top of the leader board.

He was due home that night – and home he went.

His neighbour, John Guerin, turned professional and served for a while with Henry Cotton himself.

Somehow I always felt that John's heart wasn't fully in the game; I lost trace of him – as far as I know, he is back in Killarney.

I have lost track of Bridget Gleeson too; about ten years ago she was the girl wonder.

Pat Mulcaire, whom I am privileged to number among my friends, never in his life had a lesson in golf – but this did not prevent him from winning glory in The Walker Cup.

A friend of mine who isn't short of a few pounds offered to sponsor him as a professional – but golf for Pat was always only a game.

I understood; yesterday not for the first time I realised that it's a hard way to make a living.

As I watched some famous professionals struggle, I said to myself: "It's summer time but the living isn't easy."

And while I am at it, I must also congratulate the good people of the Portmarnock Golf Club for the friendliness and competence of their organisation.

I felt in such form about tea-time that I decided to walk back to Dublin – I didn't get past Campion's.

Wednesday, June 28, 1989

Balgriffin, gateway to lovely links

Of course the word 'small' is relative – and yet we must concede that in global terms ours is a little island; in a sense, however, it is large; its diversity gives it a sense of infinite amplitude – there are parts of this country where you can feel estranged a few miles from your own home.

Balgriffin, for instance, is only a few miles from Donnycarney – and yet the city might belong to a different planet.

The narrow roads and the lush hedgerows and the proliferation of bird life combine to give a sense of countryside so deep that the signposts seem outrageous liars.

And the traffic lights at Balgriffin Cross seem as incongruous as a double-decker bus in Knocknagoshel High Street.

I have long tended to distrust people who boast of being born again but last Thursday afternoon I was inclined to relent as I felt a change coming over myself.

Several factors contributed to this harmless revolution: the links at Portmarnock is a world of wonder; the weather was glorious; the big crowd were in a kind of holiday mood which created a lovely atmosphere – and I had the good fortune to follow a trio who served up splendid golf.

I love watching people who do things well; it is a rare experience in this Ireland of ours today – but Philip Walton and Jose Maria Olazabal and Mark McNulty hovered on the brink of perfection on Thursday.

And between strokes there was so much to contemplate that the senses and the mind were suffused.

And I was in the mood to forgive anyone who might speak about the infinite variety of Portmarnock's charms.

For a start, the great links is an excellent subject for a geological thesis.

An expert on The Sahara tells me that most of its bigger sand-dunes grew up around some such object as a rock or the remains of a camel or an abandoned vehicle; I couldn't even speculate about the origin of Portmarnock's humps and mounds.

A botanist too could revel there: some parts are almost barren; other parts are so prolific that you wish you had brought a handbook.

I loved especially the little violets that flourish there in the sheltered nooks and the daisies that are almost as tiny s those that proliferate on Epsom Downs.

And then there is that great sweep of sandy shore; the tide was in on Thursday afternoon – everything was right.

And the unwonted weather seemed to be casting out inhibitions; for instance, I encountered Ranelagh's most dignified publican going around stripped to the waist.

I met another publican – among many – and he brought a little mead of consolation.

A few weeks ago on the way home – or at least back to Dublin – from New York I was in a kind of dream state and got on a bus at Dublin Airport which bore me deep into the countryside.

I wasn't unduly worried; after all, this country is a rather smallish island and so I couldn't got too far astray.

And indeed I was rather glad of my little misadventure when beyond Swords we came to a new village called River Valley; to me it seemed a portent of to-morrow's brave young Ireland.

And there I saw what appeared to be an outsize public house – it was captioned 'The Millennium'.

Time, as is its wont, went by – and I began to half-believe that River Valley existed only in my imagination and that The Millennium was but a figment.

And then near the eighteenth green on Thursday a pleasant-faced young man introduced himself as Kevin Raftery, confessed that he was mine host of The Millennium and invited me to sample its delights.

I will – some day. I hadn't a bite or a sup at Portmarnock; I was too interested in the play.

I have spent many a long day angling – sometimes from before dawn until after dusk – and wouldn't dream of taking even a morsel of food or a thimble of liquid with me to the river.

When a hen is hatching, she has only a minuscule interest in food and drink – I know how she feels.

And I was rather amused by a piece in a recent number of The Sunday Times magazine; it purported to tell you how to prepare for a day's fishing.

"I carry a small thermos of warming soup, filling Cornish pasties, a piece of juicy fruit, and a pocketful of nuts and raisins and a hip flask of Rusty Nail*."

This is for fishing on a river; for fishing from a boat you'd need "soup and coffee, pies, pastries, chunky sandwiches, hunks of cheese and fruitcake, apples and pears and home-made biscuits". The stomach boggles, not to mention the boat.

The writer, Maxine Clark, follows up with advice about how to cook your trout; it takes up several paragraphs; some people have a genius for complicating things.

Include Philip Walton out; simplicity is the basis of his game; he doesn't over-rehearse his strokes or prowl around the greens as if looking for lurking adders.

There was a holiday atmosphere at large in the great links on Thursday but for the contenders it was work as usual – and nerve-boggling and soul-testing work it is.

When you follow golfers for a round, you begin to feel a kinship with them – and so I took a special interest in Walton and Olazabal and McNulty in the subsequent days.

Of course I was especially interested in the young man from Malahide; on the only occasion I met him it was friendship at first sight.

In St. Conleth's Park on Sunday 'the busy whisper circling round' kept us intimately acquainted with the scene at Portmarnock.

Of course the result brought a feeling of anti-climax – but Philip can look back on Carrolls' '89 as his best tournament since he turned professional.

Mark McNulty finished joint third – and Olazabal ended up sixth. They got their share of the colossal money that is in golf today.

Christy O'Connor, senior, didn't do too badly; he earned about two and a half thousand.

For those who didn't make the cut it was a fruitless venture; that's the logic of the game – folklore tells us that when Ian Woosnam first played at Portmarnock, he could just about afford to stay in a B. and B.

I conducted my post-round analysis in the quiet confines of Campion's, an establishment famous for its old-fashioned character – in simple language, it is also a grocery where you can buy such goodies as jelly and custard and black and white puddings.

I was very happy there but I must confess that Campion's lacks the authentic mark of the traditional pub-cum-grocery or grocery-cum-pub; no bicycle tyres and tubes hang from its ceiling.

That, I suppose, is a reflection of the motor age.

There is another characteristic which seems to have vanished too. Who remembers the flowery pint jugs of jam, sealed with butter-paper and rubber bands?

They were, I suspect, designed as peace offerings – I knew some houses that never lacked for jugs.

*Whiskey laced with Drambuie.

Bastille Day 1989

Bicycles rule, not footballs.

Long, long ago when I worked near Hastings in the fair county of Sussex, I found many good reasons for having the odd drink in The Palace Bar, a splendid establishment on the seafront.

One reason was that from it you could see the lights on the coast of

France; to me that sight was the quintessence of romance.

In due course I came to know (kind of) the country that Caesar believed could be divided in three parts – and for once the reality matched the dream.

I love France – and with an utterly unsentimental affection; love, as W. B. Yeats used to stress, is not blind – it is fiercely perceptive.

The French have a genius for making the best of life; the most obvious example is perhaps their cooking; the kitchen mark of their cuisine is the ability to create memorable meals from moderate ingredients.

And sensible people that they are, they do not give sport a high place in the school curriculum.

That is among the reasons why in soccer and in rugby they exhibit so much imagination; it hasn't been drummed out of them by bellowing coaches.

Neither game could be described as the country's predominant sport – that honour belongs to cycling.

We first became acutely aware of this when the great, ill-fated Shay Elliott took his wares abroad.

A generation ago he led for several stages in The Tour of France; predictably he fell back in the mountains – but Shaymo had made his mark.

He proved that an Irishman could not only survive but thrive in cycling's fiercest crucible; Sean Kelly hinted strongly that an Irishman could win The Tour; Stephen Roche did it.

In that same generation we had another sporting contact with La Belle France. It took place in the C.I.E. garage in Donnybrook – our British brethren said it was an obvious site for a fight.

There a young man from Derry named Billy Kelly battled for fifteen three-minute rounds with a crafty veteran from Paris named Ray Famechon: the prize was the European featherweight title – it went to France.

And, of course, we had long been playing France annually in rugby – and occasionally in soccer. One of my French rugby heroes was a decidedly eccentric man named Alfred Roques.

Well, he was eccentric by Irish standards; here was a prop-forward who believed that he was as good a footballer as his alleged betters behind the scrum.

He dared to run and pass and even kick; for poor stultified Irish props it was a revelation.

For good measure the bould Roques didn't take up rugby until he was 32 – it could happen only in France.

France have consistently been the leading rugby power in the northern hemisphere; we have much to learn from them – but we are not learning. We are burdened with discredited theories and woefully devoid of imagination. The French, for example, think nothing of playing a lock (number 8) in the second row; such an act of heresy here would cause horror in Dublin Four and beyond.

I well remember an afternoon at Lansdowne Road when we saw an example of the French genius for adapting at its best.

Their out-half was injured; there were no replacements in those days; their great lock, Jean Prat, came out of the pack and played at out-half as if it had always been his position.

I have a special memory too of a soccer encounter with France in Paris; I wasn't present – and therein lies a little story.

I was down below in Tralee at the races and went up to my favourite village to watch the match.

Next day the startled readers of the Evening Press saw two pieces on the game; one was headed 'FROM MEL MOFFAT IN PARIS'; the other was headed 'FROM CON HOULIHAN IN KNOCKNAGOSHEL.'

France, incidentally, won 2-0, helped by an opening goal that was typical of the Giles era; our lads knocked the ball around in front of their own posts; a Frenchman nipped in – and without saying 'Merci Monsieurs' put it into the net.

Of course, we will always remember Michel Platini and his marvellous class of '82.

Perhaps the greatest display ever given by The Republic was against them at Lansdowne Road in the qualifying round for the Spanish finals.

Eoin Hand's warriors carved out a marvellous 3-2 victory; The Republic finished level on points with France but lost out on goal difference.

In the finals France had everything but luck; the gods – not to mention the referee and his linesmen – did them no favours that scorching night in Seville.

I am not prejudiced against West Germany or against East Germany but I was close to tears when France lost out in that tumultuous semi-final.

A few months later I suffered similar devastation when Seamus Darby guillotined Kerry's dream of the five-in-a-row, but it was no worse than I experienced that night in Seville – as I have said, I love France.

Friday, July 14, 1989

Bogged down in Kerry

Believe it or not – in Dublin on weekdays you can buy about twenty newspapers in the English (kind of) language, not counting in such specialist publications as The Sporting Life and The Beekeepers' Clarion and Advertiser.

I buy at least ten every day; the quiver includes The Cork Examiner and The Sporting Life – and for obvious reasons.

The Examiner is not only a fine paper; it keeps us southern exiles in touch with our roots.

The Sporting Life does its job superbly – and its letter page is invariably a joy.

People ask me how can I read ten papers a day; the answer is simple – I don't.

I doubt if anyone – except in special circumstances – reads a paper from masthead to colophon. Most of us tend to be selective.

And because the news differs little from paper to paper, you needn't read that section in them all.

And, at least as far as I am concerned, there are certain features that can be skipped.

For instance, if someone writes an article about what the well-dressed man is wearing this summer, I tend to pass.

And if I come to an article which purports to predict the state of the economy in five years time, I give it a miss – unless I am in dire need of a laugh.

For me the most fascinating items in the papers are the league tables, especially those showing the four divisions in English football.

I can ponder over those for hours, more so than ever now because of the play-offs for promotion and relegation.

I said something a while ago about special circumstances; I will give you an example.

Let us suppose that you are all on your own some day in the bog – that would constitute a special circumstance.

You have started about seven; by eleven you feel that you have earned a mug of tea plus a few sandwiches.

And so you gather a few pieces of bogdeal and light ciarans and assemble them in a little pyramid with the wood in the bottom.

Then you roll a piece of paper into a kind of fuse and ignite it – within a minute that pyramid becomes a pyre.

Now you're away in a hack; the next step is to put full-blown sods around the tabloid fire.

Then you go to the well and fill your kettle; unless you meet some damsel – it has been known to happen – you should find the fire nearing its peak when you return.

Then you plant your crozier firmly in the middle of the conflagration – I will explain.

It isn't the kind of crozier that Saint Patrick carried around with him; it is a short length of iron from which you hang the kettle.

You cannot buy this most useful artefact in the shops – but a blacksmith will make you one while you are reciting the first five verses of Gray's Elegy.

I know that blacksmiths are about as common in Ireland now as nightingales but my old friend and schoolmate, Danny Walsh, is still tending the flame below in Castle Island.

It was he who made our crozier – and many is the kettle of tea it helped to brew.

The crozier isn't essential but it is very useful; if you put the kettle on to the fire, it flattens it – and the flames go around to the outside.

When you use the crozier, the flames remain in the middle. And not only is this method more effective, you have the pleasure of watching the pyre.

Next you proceed to the sandwiches. In our household the practice was to wrap them in butter paper with a page or two of The Irish Press on the outside.

Soon the kettle is uttering steam – it is a lovely sight.

You shouldn't, however, be in a hurry, no matter how much you are in need of sustenance.

Wait until the lid begins to bobble; then the water is well and truly boiled.

There is a myth about tea in the bog – that it is very strong; the cliche says that you could trot a mouse across it.

The truth is that the tea in the bog is no different from tea elsewhere; if someone likes it strong, he waits until it has been allowed to draw beyond the average.

And of course tastes differ about sandwiches too; some people like scrambled eggs as filler; some prefer ham; some love cheese; some have a passion for bacon.

Most ham these days is a joke – indeed so is most bacon; long ago it was the custom to cure your own pork; gone are the joys.

That's all another story – let us return to the pages of newspapers on a day when you are all alone in the bog.

Believe me, no matter what the items – even articles about what the well-dressed man is wearing – you will read every word.

Of course if the pages happened to be devoted to sport, I would read every word anyway – but I would read the financial pages with almost equal avidity.

And thus one night in Hussey's pub* I astounded an American tourist, not to mention his good wife.

Americans, whether at home or abroad, have an endless need to be loved – and our visitors lost no time in getting involved in the general conversation.

The male of the species told of how glad he was to be away from Wall Street for a few weeks – he was a real live stockbroker.

I had come down from Dublin on the previous day and had just come back from the bog; I had been all on my own – and the outside wrapping of the sandwiches came from the Paris edition of The Herald Tribune.

And I gave the good man a succinct summary of what was going on in the street named after a fortification that was built to keep out the Indians.

And for good measure I informed him about the state of basketball in his native land and added a few snippets about what was happening in golf.

On that night long ago I was less than impeccably turned out – and I can still see the good wife looking at me as if saying to herself: "What manner of man is this?"

Of course I miss the bog and of course I miss the fishing – and, believe me, I am not overprone to nostalgia.

In the bog when the weather was fine and the company was good, the day flew.

And sport, of course, figured large in the conversation – and especially the state of Kerry's Gaelic football team.

In the context of that team I have one especial memory.

It concerns a September Saturday long ago; it had been a broken summer – and the turf had gone late.

And that Saturday we were determined to finish the drawing out because there were abundant signs that rain wasn't far away.

There were two of us and a half-bred mare; both she and my companion have long since gone to their eternal reward.

We started about six; it was dark when we put the last sod on the rick.

Then we hurried home, had a bite and a sup, made ourselves reasonably presentable, got on our bikes and hit off for Farranfore.

Thence 'the ghost train' bore us not so swiftly to the capital – where, I regret to say, our moral support did not bring victory to our warriors.

On that long-gone but far-from-forgotten day in the bog I saw a local belief clearly exemplified.

My neighbours – at least in the old days – had infinite faith in animals descended from the famous Arab sires that are the foundation of The Stud Book.

And that day up in Fahaduff mountain our steed, a lovely bay, put in about fourteen hours of heavy work – and then took us four miles home at a spanking rate.

And I quoted to myself the local dictum – "You can't bate the blood." Indeed...

* In Castle Island's Latin Quarter.

———

Friday, July 28, 1989

Winter school

About 25 minutes and 17 seconds past two of the clock on Wednesday the 26th of July I was accosted by one of my few remaining friends and he said: "In the name of God, what's after happening you?"

This encounter – in case you'd like to know – took place in the afternoon rather than in the small hours; the place was Merrion Row in the city of Dublin.

We adjourned to O'Donoghue's and there I spun a tale: I was, I pretended, still suffering from the fall-out engendered by the Munster final.

I doubted if he would believe the truth; about an hour previously I had read an article on Dublin by an English journalist which didn't mention Mulligan's, The Long Hall, or The Brazen Head.

Otherwise it was par for the course: there was the usual guff about the great conversation in the pubs, the proliferation of dark-eyed colleens, and the excellence of a named brown stout.

And of course there was a great passage about certain writers and artists who have given rise to the cliche _ "There are no characters left."

I was acquainted in varying degrees with most of those alleged characters – and, believe me, they were people whom you wouldn't take home to your granny or even to your great-granny.

If a character is someone who 'borrows' money from you and then proceeds to bore the trousers off you, they are not scarce in The Republic's capital.

And of course in that aforementioned article there was the statutory homage to James Joyce.

The old artificer has no greater admirer than I – but there is a difference between admiration and adulation.

I despise those people – and they are not thin on the ground – who deem every word he wrote as sacred.

In my not-so-humble opinion our Jim's reputation must rest on 'Dubliners' and the 'Portrait'.

To condemn 'Ulysses' is about as foolhardy as casting aspersions on The Book of Kells or The Dingle Dolphin or Sean Kinsella's cooking or the Artane Boys' Band – but I must confess that the alleged Great Irish

Novel never moved me.

I have long felt is contained too much head and too little heart; at least to me, 'Sons And Lovers' makes it look like a tediously contrived concoction.

And to deem it an accurate reproduction of Dublin on a certain day is rather naive; our Jim didn't even get the winner of The Gold Cup right.

'Ulysses' is, however, a mansend to thesis hunters; sometimes I wonder how our scholarly neighbours across the Atlantic would survive without it.

Doctorates have been spawned by studies of merely sections of it.

I have seen essays devoted to single paragraphs of it – and I find this exhilaratingly funny; it is hardly a secret that 'Ulysses' is riddled with misprints.

There is a Joyce Summer School at large in Dublin these days; I wonder will anyone stand up and utter even a tiny criticism of the old artificer.

I doubt it: he or she would risk defenestration – or drowning in a duckpool if the business is on the ground floor*.

Now I see that The Abbey are about to stage all of W.B. Yeats's plays – God between us and all harm.

Ould Willie knew as much about drama as I do about aerobics. Let it pass – there is no arguing against fashion.

And that brings us to more serious matters, including the general attitude towards my native county.

I am not referring to the myth that every Kerry person is a born footballer; that subject is at present too painful – my complaint is rooted elsewhere.

I love the Dingle peninsula and I have spent many a happy day in the Barony of Iveragh but I wish those who write about travel and tourism would realise that there are other regions to explore in The Kingdom.

The term 'Ring of Kerry' symbolises the general attitude: it isn't the ring of Kerry – it is the ring of South Kerry.

One day some travel writer will discover the great moorland that extends north from a few miles above Castle Island to near Listowel – and west from Knocknagoshel to within a few miles of The Atlantic.

John B. Keane will tell you how much it influenced him; of course it did – he can hardly write an article without mentioning Renagown or Lyrecrompane.

I have never seen it mentioned in any of those guides issued by the various tourist bodies.

All these worthy people seem fixed in their views: according to them the real Ireland is along by the coast, preferably in the west.

Believe me, the inland parts of the country are real too, sometimes alarmingly so.

If you happen to be in West Munster, you might do worse then venture into the great moorland.

It is a lonely world in winter but in early April it comes alive.

Then the pink-and-white of the flowering currant begins to decorate the hedges; work commences on the bog; the larks rise up out of the heather and sing for the sheer heaven of it.

Many people seem to look on sunbathing on some Mediterranean beach as the ideal holiday – count me out.

I have never taken a holiday – and I can imagine no better recreation than a fine day in the bog.

It is no place for the dilettante but if you fall in love with it – as I did at first sight – you will quickly learn the relevant skills.

And when you pour the remains of the tea over the embers as you prepare to go home in the evening, you will experience a moment of especial loneliness.

The moorland breeds a hardy people but very few go in for Gaelic football or any football; they just couldn't afford to break a bone in the days between early April and October.

Eddie Walsh, the great Kerry wing-half-back, came from the moorland but he was a special case; he worked as a timekeeper with the county council – and it didn't matter much if he broke a bone, even one of his own.

Jerry Kiernan, the celebrated long-distance runner, grew up in Brosna, on the eastern verge of that great expanse of bog and little fields.

And John Lenihan, great but more or less unsung, is another man whose matrix was the moorland.

John lives in Bearnageeha, The Windy Gap. He belongs to the parish of Ballymacelligot but has always been deemed a Castle Island man.

We have excellent grounds for claiming him: Ballymacelligot is a huge parish but doesn't contain a town or even a village; for the Lenihan family The Island has always been their place for selling and buying.

And John runs for An Ríocht, the club that fights out of my home town.

Now I will tell you a strange little story; two Sundays ago John competed in an exceptionally prestigious race; on Monday morning I searched the Irish papers for the result – in vain.

And so I was especially delighted when I saw my neighbour's name in a headline in The Daily Telegraph.

The event was the celebrated Snowdon Race at Llanberis in North Wales; if you labelled it the hill runners' European Championship, you wouldn't be far out.

The course is about five miles up and the same distance down, The field of over 800 included the famous Swiss runner, Martin May, and the English star, Malcolm Patterson.

John was second in his only other run in this race – that was three years ago. This time he finished 300 yards ahead of Patterson; May came in third.

It was a wonderful performance from a full-time farmer. It should have made the front pages here on the Monday – amazingly, it didn't make any pages atall.

John turned out for Sligo's Warriors' Race up and down Knocknarea last Friday evening – and galloped away with it.

A few years ago he led for much of the way in the Dublin City Marathon - but even John's mighty heart couldn't fight off the cramp that assailed him a few miles from the finishing line.

Anyhow, he and Jerry Kiernan and John Griffin have shown the world that there is more to Kerry than football and fishing and 'traditional' music and ancient storytellers and mad bodhran makers and luscious black puddings and dark-eyed colleens wishing you the top of the evening.

*I have no objection to summer schools – but I would welcome a winter school where honest criticism might get a peep-in.

Wednesday, August 2, 1989

The days of port and periwinkles

About tea-time last Friday two words jumped up out of this paper and smote me; suddenly I realised that high summer is almost past – the words were 'Market Rasen."

That strange name has an especial place in the lore of the turf: it symbolises the world of humble racing which underpins the sport of kings.

Market Rasen is in Lincolnshire, the flattest county in all of England, so low-lying that it will be inundated when the Arctic icecap melts.

I would love to know what 'Rasen' signifies; I have asked some of my scholarly friends but got only speculation.

It isn't the only occurrence of that word in Lincolnshire's place-names; nearby are West Rasen and Middle Rasen.

Will someone please tell me what 'Rasen' means? It is a lovely word and that makes it all the more tantalising.

Does anyone – apart from myself – remember Jean Ingelow?

She was once Lincolnshire's most famous daughter; her poem 'The High Tide On The Coast Of Lincolnshire' used to be a great favourite with anthologists.

 The county's most notorious daughter is the woman who seems purgatory-bent on leading her people into the past.

I doubt if Margaret Thatcher ever went to Market Rasen races or to any races; perhaps such frivolity is beneath her.

Anyhow, the little track is getting on without her presence – and its card for last Saturday was of the kind which is more or less the staple diet of those who love the National Hunt.

There were two handicap chases – one of two miles and one of three; there was a novice chase; there was a handicap hurdle and a selling hurdle – and of course there was a maiden hurdle.

And of course it attracted by far the biggest field of the day.

My definition of an incorrigible optimist is someone who bets on maiden hurdles; you might as well be having a wager on which steer will be the last rounded up in a stampede.

Market Rasen is far from the world of the sheikhs and Vincent O'Brien and Robert Sangster, not to mention Henry Cecil and Guy Harwood and

Michael Stoute – and none the worse for that.

Nevertheless, some lively betting went on there last Saturday; The Sporting Life is my authority.

For example, in the first race, a two-mile handicap chase, Taffy Jones opened at 11/10 and attracted bets of £550, £500, £400, £300 and eventually a stream of late office money.

His price fluctuated between 5/4 and the ultimate odds of 10/11; obviously it was a strong market when such big bets caused so little difference.

His backers had little to worry about: "Always handy, led going well three out, ran on strongly in the run-in." In fact, he won by five lengths.

There was even bolder wagering in the novices' chase; someone had £1,000 to win £1,625 on Ben Ledi; he opened at 11/8 and at the off was 6/4.

A novices' chase is an excellent medium for relieving a punter of his money; the favourite, though partnered by the excellent Mark Dwyer, bit the turf. The winner, All Hello, opened at 6/1 and was returned at eights.

And seemingly there were a few incorrigible optimists at Market Rasen on Saturday; the maiden hurdle attracted a lively market.

Whitehouse Gem opened at 11/8, hardly an attractive price in a field of nineteen.

Among the bets she attracted were £800 to win £1,200 – and £800 to win £1,000. The off price was 6/4.

The favourite didn't live up to her name; she finished a well-beaten third. She too was partnered by Mark Dwyer. The close-up tells us that she was always well placed but failed to quicken from the last.

Some strange things happened in that same maiden hurdle: Mig, for instance, whipped round at the start and unseated Robert Marley; Forever Tingo tried to refuse at the second and was eventually pulled up by Dermot Browne.

The Sporting Life on Monday carried a little feature on the Market Rasen meeting.

It tells us about a 23-year-old named Guy Upton; he partnered the aforementioned Taffy Jones.

Young Upton has nineteen wins to his credit and can have six more before he loses his five pounds' allowance.

Steve Boggett, the author of the piece, says that Guy is a very determined young man – we'll be watching out for him.

Incidentally, the aforementioned Ben Ledi is trained by Jonjo O'Neill; Steve tells us that he jumped spectacularly and was leading by four lengths when he touched down too steeply four out. We'll be watching him too.

An intriguing item in the little piece concerns a man called Ray Bostock; he had his first winner as a trainer at Market Rasen on Saturday.

There is nothing remarkable about that – until you learn that he is a solicitor who has closed his office and set up a small yard.

Meanwhile back here at home it is the high season of the flapping game, a sub-world that attracts big crowds but rarely gets mentioned in the morning papers.

It surfaced for a while a few years when a racing journalist of the investigative breed almost threw up his type-writer in horror at the thought of certain goings-on in that most democratic of sporting arenas.

I was slightly shocked because he was shocked: horses from under the rules have been running in the flappers since racing first began.

And indeed it is not unknown for the odd jockey from the up-market scene to partner a mount in the arena where they race around the poles.

One day long ago when I worked for another paper, I happened to come across a well-known jockey at Dingle races.

He was disguised in the darkest of glasses as he made his way to the enclosure to partner an outsider in a fairly big race.

And he said to me: "In the honour of God, don't mention my name to anyone."

I guaranteed him that there wasn't the slightest danger – and he said: "I know that – and don't tell anyone but we'll be trying for our life."

That in simple language meant that his mount was off – or in simpler language that he would be ridden to win. He was – and he did.

I miss the flapping circuit: it was nice to be a biggish fish in a smallish pool.

And the very word 'flapper' conjures up in my mind's nose a marvellously distinctive smell.

It was compounded of fresh bread and newly-cut ham and seagrass and periwinkles and equine sweat and bruised grass and hoof-indented turf; Chanel - which is made from roses and jasmine – couldn't compete.

And in my mind's eye I see the bar-tent: the counter was made up of planks on tar-barrels; there was no lounge – and the stock was basic; it usually consisted of no more than bottled beer and stout and whiskey and brandy and minerals.

At the more ambitious meetings you might find sherry and a certain drink which in most places is called port but which in Kerry a generation ago was invariably called port wine.

And I miss the conniving and the conspiring and the double and even the treble dealing; the flapping world makes Machiavelli seem like a kinsman of Candide.

I have never been to the races at Market Rasen, except in my daydreams. It is an ambition I cherish.

Some day I hope to visit that modest track which has the shortest run-in of any course in these islands.

I have a few other cherished ambitions too.

I would love to see the source of the mighty Loire – it comes out of a wooden pipe in a farmer's yard in the hills of Eastern France; I long to see the brent geese making their annual pilgrimage to The Shetlands; I would love to hear the nightingale, not necessarily in Berkeley Square; some day I hope to see the elephant in his native habitat – I must hurry as it seems that the ivory hunters will wipe the species out; I would love to see the vines growing on some south-facing slope in deepest Kerry and sample Lyrecrompane '99; some day perhaps I will enjoy a few tins of Foster's in the shadow of Ayer's Rock – and, most of all, before I shuffle off the mortal coil, I would dearly love to see the footballers of a certain county on a September Sunday in a field in Dublin Three.

'Rasen', I have discovered, means 'river'.

Friday, August 11, 1989

Free enterprise in the turf world

A few days ago I suggested that the Keady case could end up in the civil courts; now I see that John Bowles is thinking about challenging The Jockey club in The Court Of Human Rights.

Mr. Bowles, as far as I know, has never played hurling either here or in America – but nevertheless he is a notable exponent of free enterprise.

In a selling hurdle at Newton Abbot away back in 1978 he brought off a famous – or notorious – coup by the oldest trick in the business; he ran a ringer.

The horse in the racecard was named In The Money; his extended form figures were letters rather than numbers – and indicated that when he hadn't fallen, he had been pulled up or refused or merely ran out.

He was hardly the kind of nag that would entice you to have even the minimum bet – but he won going away.

In fact, he didn't win – a smart performer called Cobblers' March won in his name.

And, of course, Honest Joe and his colleagues did a song-and-dance in righteous indignation – and, of course, the stewards went into action.

Eventually the enterprising Mr. Bowles was found guilty and disqualified for twenty years.

Now you may think that 'disqualified' means that he cannot hold a trainer's licence or officially own a horse – it goes far beyond that.

A disqualified person cannot attend any meeting – Flat, National Hunt, or Point-to-Point.

John Bowles was fined £500 for attending a meeting at Cheltenham last year – and £1,000 for allegedly attending a Point-to-Point in Wales a few weeks ago.

He denies the second charge; he travelled to the meeting with a few friends but remained in the car park outside the course; the disciplinary committee accepted this – yet still fined him.

The Jockey Club has long behaved as if it is totally above the laws of the land – so much so that if they murdered someone in their offices in Portland Square, they would probably plead privilege.

To forbid a person from attending a race meeting is outrageous unless in the case of someone who is known to be violent or given to dipping a hand in other people's pockets.

The ban on John Bowles is savagely vindictive; he will be in his mid-sixties before he can watch a race in the flesh again – unless he wins in the civil court.

It is a cruel punishment, even for a Welshman.

And it serves no purpose – except as a warning to others.

It doesn't prevent Mr. Bowles from attempting another coup – to do so he needn't be present in the flesh.

Will someone explain why employing a ringer is more heinous than stopping a horse?

We all know that steeds are occasionally kept under wraps in several races and produced on the 'right' occasion – it is more or less taken for granted.

And the stewards rarely act unless it has been done too blatantly – and when the culprits are found guilty, the penalty is very light compared to that inflicted on John Bowles.

And yet to me this practice is more offensive than employing a ringer – because it deceives the public in not one but in several races.

And even though the enterprising Welshman has been disqualified for a score of years, you can be sure that none of his neighbours and friends think any the worse of him.

Let us be honest about it, although 'honest' in this context may seem a rather strange word: racing has its own ethical code.

I am well acquainted with some of the people who organised – or disorganised – the Gay Future affair; they haven't fallen a centimetre in my estimation.

Well, in a sense they have: I wouldn't entrust them with the robbing of an orchard.

The Gay Future affair was a comedy of errors.

It began on the Saturday night before the August Bank Holiday when the man entrusted with the care of the horse arrived in Cartmel.

The horse was supposed to be in training in Scotland; his handler came from Ireland; that night he adjourned to a pub frequented by racing men – and asked where he could get Mass in the morning.

You could hardly say that he was keeping a low profile.

And just to maintain the high profile, no less a man than my old friend Timmy Jones was the chosen pilot.

And, of course, as the whole world knows, the two horses named with Gay Future weren't even in training.

They were above in a lush Ayrshire pasture, so fat with grass that they could hardly raise a gallop for a furlong.

And just to make things even crazier, the two lads in charge of the horseless horse-box dallied at a roadside café and left at an hour when they couldn't get to their intended destinations in time.

It was some coup – that's for sure – but at least it added to the gaiety of nations and produced a good book and an enchanting movie.

Coups are as much a part of racing as yeast is of brown stout.

I see nothing immoral in them – because between the bookmakers and the punters there are no holds barred.

The bookies too pull strokes but we don't hear so much about them.

Putting up a false favourite is a familiar ploy; the innocents who think that a short price indicates a flood of money are the victims.

I suspect that there was an example at Galway last week.

And, of course, most of the big bookmakers maintain an intelligence network made up of jockeys and stable lads.

And, of course, they do not hesitate to take money on a horse which they know isn't 'off' – that's part of the other side of the coin.

By now the innocent reader may have begun to suspect that racing is about as bent as stock jobbing.

Of course it has its elements of inside trading but it couldn't survive if it happened to be as corrupt as some people think.

Proverbially there is honour among thieves; within racing's peculiar code there are stringent laws too.

And in this context I am reminded of something that belongs to the lore of the flapping world.

One time long ago a certain Corkman acquired a few very useful horses and joined the circuit.

He belonged to The Church of Ireland – and therein lies the tale.

He was a most moral man – and slowly it dawned on the others in the circuit that he was always out to win.

They hoped that in time he would see the light and come around to their way of thinking.

And things, as the man said, eventually reached a head.

The head conspirator at the time was a great friend of mine – but even though he is long since gone to his grave, I will refrain from naming him.

Anyhow on the night before our local meeting he offered the newcomer more than the value of the morrow's big race if he would play ball.

Fifty pounds was a fair lump of money thirty years ago but the honest newcomer said "No way".

And when my friend told the story to me, he added a rider: "Them Protestants aren't Christians atall."

Wednesday, August 16, 1989

The big game – when pressure meant steam

The unknown aphorist who first said that it is better to travel hopefully than to arrive never experienced the joys of a 36-hour flight from Gatwick to Auckland.

Nor was he ever on a war-time train from Kerry to Dublin; it was an endurance test at the best of times and especially so on the way to an All-Ireland final – then the sheer weight of the numbers slowed progress and even caused fears that the train wouldn't arrive in time.

There was no tannoy on the trains in those far-off days and whenever the not-so-sweet chariot stopped for no obvious reason, panic would begin to raise its silly head.

And aficionados – they existed before Ernest Hemingway popularised the word – would begin to worry about having to 'watch' the match on the wireless in some pub in Tipperary perhaps or in Laois or maybe in Kildare itself.

It never happened – but in quite recent times a Derby special from Tralee failed to reach The Curragh in time for the big race. Some people were rather angry.

The preparations for those war-time journeys were in proportion to the expectations of delay.

To me they will forever be associated with the smell of freshly-cut ham; it was as much part of the big games as incense is of Benediction.

And in the mind's eye I will forever see a sight that has now all but disappeared.

I see little groups of men walking steadily towards Croke Park, becapped and solidly shod, topcoat slung over one shoulder and a big brown-paper-covered parcel firmly clutched.

They were the grassroots of the G.A.A., men who lived in a world where such words as 'motivation' and 'commitment' were unknown.

The word 'pressure' was at large but referred mainly to steam engines.

Now the comments before big games – in all codes – are littered with those three words.

You hear of players being not only under pressure but under extra pressure.

And, of course, the accursed media are blamed by some people for unseemly incidents on-and-off the pitch.

It is forgotten by the media bashers that not all war-time big games were graceful affairs – indeed the football All-Ireland final of 1943 could charitably be described as a thundering disgrace.

The media barely existed then: there was no television; wireless sets were few; the national papers consisted of only a few sheets.

And yet the hitman went about his nefarious trade.

For far too long the G.A.A. have been very reluctant to concede that not all those who play its games are exemplary sportsmen.

There is, for example, no penalty points system as in soccer; in the G.A.A.'s scheme of things a player could be booked every Sunday and avoid suspension.

And, of course, the managerial revolution has exacerbated matters.

Occasionally you hear a manager say that he wouldn't have a hitman on his team; perhaps there are a few who are as good as their word.

I fear, however, that the majority have such a lust to win that their consciences become rather flexible in the context of sport.

Let us speak of better things; since I made the hegira to Dublin, I miss a few aspects of rural life.

The fishing is one; I am a member of a Dublin club but its rules restrict you to two trout per day.

I am afraid that I'm not yet ready for such a rigid regime.

And I miss "coming up for the match"; when the car began to proliferate, the journey could be a pleasure.

I have pleasant memories of making little fires on The Curragh and boiling the water and frying the black puddings.

It wasn't only Napoleon Bonaparte who believed that an army travels on its stomach.

It must be admitted, however, that the homeward journey could be tiresome – especially if your warriors had gone under.

For most of us then the idea of spending Sunday night in Dublin was a non-starter; work beckoned – and beckoned rather sternly.

Of course, the temptation to stay could be almost overpowering but you would feel very guilty if you broke the peasant code.

I have a special memory of the night after Dublin had beaten Galway in the All-Ireland final of 1963.

I was in O'Donoghue's, not then as famous as it is now but, nevertheless, a lively establishment.

I was in fair company: It included Sean Ó Murchú, Seamus Ennis, Ted Furey (yes, the dad), Aindreas Ó Gallchoir, and my travelling companions, the two Riordan brothers from Scartaglen.

Of course, all three of us would love to have stayed but, of course, we didn't.

The two lads had to be back at McElligott's garage in the morning; I had promised to take a few cattle to the fair with a neighbour.

The same neighbour's fences were not in the best of repair – and rounding up his bullocks in the dark of the pre-morning was not a congenial task for someone who wasn't in the best of repair himself.

On that Monday long ago I was – as they used to say in the country – 'hanging on by a thread'.

I had almost forgotten that phrase until a few days ago – it surfaced in a delightful letter from Ian Lee, a scholarly man who runs his godly race in Collins Lane, Tullamore, the capital of a county which I love.

Ian was sunning himself on the beach at Curracloe in deepest South-East Wexford when a back page of this paper drifted his way.

It included my oul'column; it was a piece mainly about the cutting of turf.

Ian writes that although the taste of the sea was in his mouth, he could instantly smell the bog.

"I could see bog cotton, hear the squelch of bare feet – and taste my mother's egg sandwiches."

Ian goes on: "Many's the time I made the daily stroll to the well with a gallon can bought from a good old-fashioned tinker..."

And that day below in Curracloe a certain occasion came back to him with especial vividness.

"My neighbours – some of them long since gone – were there.

"Jack Hannify was on the slean – and not in the best of shape.

"My father, gladly still fit and able to go to the bog, was fixing poor Jack with a look not a bit sympathetic and urging him to throw out the last few precious sods before the water rushed in, the dam broke, or the whole bog caved in."

Ian says: "In those far-off days I didn't understand the effects of a night drinking porter in Finlay's of Mount Bolus had on a turf-cutting performance."

And how did Jack Hannify reply to the urgings of Ian's da?

– "Dear God, Lee, I'm hanging on by a thread."

Friday, August 25, 1989

'Wicket' season for England

Estyn Evans who departed this earthly world a few days ago was as wise a man as ever came out of Wales – and that is saying a great deal.

I never met him but I read all his books and they immensely enriched me; he was a great geographer in the fullest sense of the word.

The geography that most of us acquired at school wasn't too bad; at least it gave us a fair idea of how the land and the water lie.

And we learned about the cotton towns of Lancashire and the wool towns of Yorkshire – and we discovered to our delight and astonishment that most of the needles used by our mothers and sisters were made in a little town called Redditch.

We didn't, however, learn much about our own country or our own townlands; we weren't encouraged to look around us and ask, for example, why some hedges were straight lines and others so crooked that they seemed to have been plotted by a madman.

Estyn Evans followed what is known as the French humanist concept of geography – at least as much as a Welshman can follow anything.

This essentially is about the relationship between man and his environment – and of course it embraces what we have come to know as history; the truth is that history and geography are one.

History, as most of us learned it, is mainly concerned with politics, with broad movements that visibly bring about change; of day to day life we found out little.

Estyn Evans spent most of his working life in Belfast and of course was acutely aware of its tribal tensions; in hardly any other part of the world was there greater need to dispel myth and establish truth.

This island is woefully bedevilled by myths; what is – wrongly perhaps – labelled the Christian Brothers' concept of history is about as veracious as the popular image of how The West was won.

The glorification of The Gael was akin to the Nazis' 'theory of Aryan superiority but it must be admitted that not all its consequences were sinister – some were rather hilarious.

I am thinking especially of the infamous Ban promulgated by The Gaelic Athletic Association; lads and lassies of this generation must find its ramifications almost incredible.

It is a topic of which I am tired; I am glad that I have lived to see the day when playing a 'foreign' game doesn't have you branded as an inferior Irishman.

Incidentally, I was saddened when I heard a few days ago that an Antrim hurling club had its goalposts cut down; that's the other side of the coin.

Not all the news is bad; cricket has been revived in my own county, probably because some enthusiasts from the sub-continent of India are working down there.

A club has sprung up in Tralee; they have played a series of matches – as yet no angry Celtic or Gaelic god has hurled a thunderbolt at the miscreants.

The ignorant who it seems will be always with us look on this ancient game as a precluse of the upper classes; it is far from it; indeed there was an era when it was banned in England because men with damaged hands were less efficient as labourers and archers.

And for long it has been as much the game of the English coalminers as rugby is of their Welsh fellows.

And in the last century and for part of this it was popular in many parts of Ireland, as students of Canon Sheehan and Francis Ledwidge know.

Then came the green deluge; all things deemed foreign were suspect; the lunacy reached its pinnacle one day in Leitrim when a big march was organised to protest against "jazz". You don't believe it.... It happened.

Cricket is a marvellous game, not least because it provides for all kinds of physical types and because you needn't put away your bat as you approach the two score.

And not the least of its appeal is its tactical depth; it makes all other field games look exceedingly simple.

A captain in cricket is rather more than someone who partakes in the toss, decides who takes the place-kicks, and offers the odd few words of encouragement: when his team are fielding, he must be as acutely aware as a hen minding chickens in a land where hawks abound.

By moving a fielder as little as a few yards he can transform the shape of a match; the tactical subtleties are infinite.

So is the variety of deliveries available to the bowlers; that department has a fascinating vocabulary.

'Chinaman' and 'yorker' and 'googly' are fairly familiar but not everybody knows what a 'bosey' is. It is an exaggerated form of the googly;

it was called after a professional cricketer named Bosanquet; you may remember one of his sons – he had a rather colourful career as a newsreader on television.

Quick bowling is dramatic, sometimes melodramatic, but the various kinds of spin are to cricket as caviare is to cuisine.

Those of us who are older remember two modest little men from the West Indies who so bewitched England a generation ago; in the process they helped their team win a series in the game's home for the first time.

They were duly immortalised in a lovely calypso; it begins "Cricket, lovely cricket at Lord's where they play it" and the chorus goes

"With those two little pals of mine,
Ramadhin and Valentine."

In the meantime the men from the West Indies have relied mainly on pace; suddenly a crop of giants seems to have sprung up amongst them – Ramadhin and Valentine appear to have come from a different world.

Once upon a time the term 'six-footer' conveyed that a man was exceptionally tall; if you happen to be in O'Connell Street at rush hour nowadays, you will see that six-footers are almost as common as daisies in a May field.

And the emergence of bowlers who are well over six feet has been a boon to makers of head gear and has prompted some gurus to suggest that the distance between the wickets should be increased.

That is unlikely to happen: it would make life too difficult for those men who depend on guile rather than pace.

Monday/Tuesday, October 31, 1989

Streets broad and narrow

Every age, as some anonymous philosopher said, has its false alarms; it is a dictum that the faint of heart tend to apply to The Dublin City Marathon.

The evidence of numbers seems to bear them out; I have heard even aficionados referring to the "good old days".

This year the entries were dramatically down; it was almost inevitable

– many people had proved to themselves and friends that they could conquer this horizontal Everest and were content to rest on their invisible laurels.

It would be rash, however, to forecast that the graph will continue its downward curve; the peak years could be compared to a river in high flood; now it is back well within its banks but could rise again.

The marathon will always have its critics, those congenital pessimists who look on even a sprint for a bus as a health hazard – but they can never prevail against the yeast of the human spirit.

Yesterday's number may have seemed small; the word is comparative – as I realised about seven past eleven yesterday morning as the human river surged into Kevin Street.

And once again I failed to pick out some friends and colleagues in the main body of the onrush.

It is no problem to discern your friends in the wheelchair race; come back, Gerry O'Rourke, with your chariot of fire.

And it is easy to pick out any friends you may have in the cerebral palsy platoon; yesterday they numbered eight.

And usually I can pick out those of the elite who are in the first ten or so; then the difficulty starts and quickly worsens.

No matter how intently you focus, you will miss many of those in whom you have a special interest – because in the first mile or so they are as closely massed as a flight of starlings.

Every year I know again and again the frustration of hearing someone call out my name and not being able to shout back "Great stuff" to Mickeen or Willie Joe or May Ellen or whomever.

Yesterday I took up my post, as distinct from An Post, at the bottom of New Bride Street.

It was a beautiful morning; the fuchsia in Heytesbury Street was in all its modest glory.

The watchers in the Kevin Street flats had a grandstand view; the pigeons on the roof were one better.

The watchers at this point were thin on the ground.

I missed the atmosphere of the old days when you could see children in arms bobbling like the lid of a boiling kettle.

Nevertheless, life went on and a few minutes after eleven the river began to rise.

Never have I seen a stranger first paragraph.

Usually at this point about ten or so of the elite come clustered.

Martin Jordan was about 50 yards ahead of the human deer known as the elite.

Even at that stage the field – or road – was strung out.

Nevertheless, the elite went by, applauded but looking as if rapt in a world of their own.

The field as always at this stage were very much aware of the watchers.

And I thought of William Wordsworth and mentally misquoted him:
"Three thousand saw I at a glance,
Tossing their heads in sprightly dance."

And when all the field had passed, I went home and put on the television and the kettle, in that order.

In all fairness to RTE (for once) they did a good job.

And Frank Greally was an inspired choice as nuts-and-bolts man.

And such is the power of the image that Dublin looked beautiful – and maybe it is.

And laden with Peter Barry's tea and excitement I went up to the canal – The Grand, in case you wish to know.

There was a mighty crowd at Harold's Cross Bridge – and all along down the canal.

The experts will tell you that this juncture plays a big part in the strategy of the marathon.

At The Bridge you are into a long house-shaded straight.

And here the contenders tend to show their hands – or perhaps their legs.

And true to theory, John Griffin and Hamilton Cox came into Grove Road on their own.

John, running on the canal side, wore a dark head-band and a green singlet; the man from Greenock was white-visored and in royal blue.

In height and build they could be twins; John was running with slightly the shorter stride.

By now it was clear that barring cramp or an attack from a mad dog it was a two-man race.

Nevertheless, the watchers as always applauded everybody; indeed they tend to adulate the elite and admire the rest.

It must be admitted, however, that the two resident swans along by Portobello Road were unmoved.

And about a hundred yards upstream a flotilla of mallard went on feeding, a reminder that the peasants of Brabant went about their work on the day of Waterloo.

I followed the people-rush all along down the canal; yesterday between walking and jogging I covered the race and about ten miles.

And though the number of participants was down to a third of the peak year, '83, the atmosphere was wonderful.

I heard my name called out at Leeson Street Bridge. Was it my old friend from Castle Island, Anthony Cronin?

By now the road was littered with drink cartons, milk in white-and-blue, Pukari in blue-and-white.

Somewhere around Leeson Street Bridge I met a lovely frenzy of people from England.

It included seven wives whose menfolk were in the run; their green-and-orange banners proclaimed 'Hunsted Harriers'.

I met them again in St. Stephen's Green; the good news is that all the seven husbands are alive and well.

By about a quarter to one I met a neighbour from home whose face was aglow; before he spoke, I guessed the news – John Griffin had broken clear.

And I was present and correct when he rounded the corner into the home straight, Stephen's Green East.

The applause was tumultuous; I shed a few tears as my great neighbour strode into his kingdom.

For a fleeting moment Our John seemed to smile; in fact, he was only squinting as he came face to face with the sun.

John is a modest as a Kerry person can be – but it must be admitted that he lengthened his stride over the last hundred yards.

And it must be stated too that the applause for Hamilton Cox, a long-striding second, was only a little less.

I am not an expert on the decibel system but I believe that the greatest applause of all was for Pauline Nolan.

The sprite from Shankhill on the outskirts of Dublin ran a magnificent race. Was it her first marathon?

All in all, it was a great day.

On the way home I was man-knapped and dragged into John Gleeson's in Portobello.

There I met my not-so-old and dear friend, John Joe Barry, who was celebrating John Griffin's victory.

Wednesday, November 1, 1989

Jim Murray sees red

Frank Greally, the pocket battleship who quit a secure job and founded Irish Runner, gets to the The United States about as often as I get to Croke Park and on most visits calls into one or other of their mighty book-marts and brings me back a present.

That is more than I do for him whenever I visit Croke Park but I'm working at it.

A few days ago he brought me 'The Jim Murray Collection'; I fell upon it like a small boy who has just bought his first comic.

Jim Murray's name may not mean anything to most people in this country; I don't think his work was ever syndicated here but on the other side of The Atlantic he dwells on the same plateau as Ring Lardner and Grantland Rice and Red Smith.

And the plateau is rather elevated and to get up there you need some talent, a child-like mind, and a mighty capacity for hard work.

And so I was especially interested in Jim Murray's piece about Red Smith, one master wordwright writing about another.

What I have long admired in American sports writers is their utter lack of begrudgery; they remind me of what some old Roman said one day long ago – "See how those Christians love one another".

I wasn't disappointed; indeed I felt like going out into the street and shouting 'Magnifico, Magnifico, Magnifico', but I refrained lest I be joined by a certain shepherd dog called Duke; he might get excited and lose the run of himself.

Jim wisely begins by examining his hero's name – 'Red' was not conferred at the baptismal font.

Indeed the infant Smith was christened Walter Wellesley, a title no doubt intended as a springboard to the worlds of stockbroking or investment banking or perhaps to The White House itself.

Jim Murray says: "He had a moniker right out of the pages of Ivanhoe and he preferred a name that sounded as if he had just climbed down from a truck."

Red Smith was born in the imperfectly-delineated region known as The Mid-West.

It gave him a head start; a remarkable number of outstanding

Americans have come from that territory where their ancestors settled when there was no more land to be acquired in the real West.

Red Smith had an excellent preparation for his calling, if calling it was; he managed to avoid much of the inflicting of knowledge that is called education and resolutely ensured that he would acquire no profession or trade.

He fished in the streams and wandered in the woods and frequented ballparks and racetracks and gymnasiums and other places that served as open universities before the term was minted.

Eventually the evil day came; he had to find some kind of gainful employment. And in the time-hallowed words 'he drifted into journalism'.

It is an odd calling: those who are best prepared for it are they who are prepared for nothing else.

Red Smith explained it rather differently, with no doubt a tongue in each cheek: "I went into the newspapers because I disliked lifting things."

He started on a modest journal called The North Michigan Pioneer and Recorder; the wages were modest too but at least he had a title – he was a copy boy.

The title was rather grandiloquent but the work was easy.

Young Smith had merely to take copy to the typesetters, make coffee about every ten minutes, go out to buy sandwiches and milk and hot dogs and cold dogs and doughnuts, run bets and various messages, and go with proofs to find sub-editors who had mysteriously gone missing and who were invariably winkled out in some establishment where fermented liquor was on tap.

The post was not without its perks: Occasionally - very occasionally – he would be assigned to cover some minor ballgame in some manforsaken neck of Upper Michigan.

Young Smith was so delirious when he got his first such assignment that he bought a portable typewriter; he bought it in a junk-shop but it was a typewriter nonetheless.

On the train back from the obscure township he lovingly condensed his thousand words into the required 500; next day it appeared as two very short paragraphs, unsigned.

Nevertheless, Red Smith was on his way; a month later he got another such assignment; this time the required 500 words came out as three paragraphs, again rather brief.

There was, however, a difference: his name was appended and he got an extra five dollars in his week's wages; it went to his head – late that night he bought a jug of beer for the chief sub-editor.

Red Smith left this mortal world in the January of 1982 – and left an abundance of little stories and quotable quotes behind him.

I love the story about the bookmaker who booked himself on an ocean liner in quarters so palatial that he found himself with a bevy of Astors and Rockefellers.

Eventually one of those top-drawer people asked him how he could afford it; the bookie, somewhat laconically, said "Odds-on favourites".

Red was also a collector of his colleagues' one-liners, including Tom Meany's description of fabled Rudy York as 'part Indian, part first baseman'.

His own analysis of Avery Brundage was not as pithy but eminently quotable.

Mr. Brundage, you will remember, seemed convinced that he, single-handed, had invented The Olympic Games.

Red Smith was not convinced: "He stood as a monument to Avery Brundage's concept of sport. It did not trouble him that what he stood for existed mainly in his own mind. And he had an integrity equalled only by his insensitivity."

Red had his own blind spots; he led the pack that pilloried Muhammad Ali when he declined to be drafted into the forces for the war in Vietnam.

Ali was the better judge of the situation; Red should have stuck to sport.

The blunder is almost forgotten now; the goodness of his writing lives after him.

He especially excelled in writing about the racetrack, not so much about great horses and trainers and jockeys as about the little people, notably the clockers, that peculiarly American element of our civilisation.

Red Smith was, of course, a first-class groupie; unlike Ring Lardner he loved the company of those people whose careers he chronicled.

Ring was a patrician; nowhere was his snobbery more blatant than in his paranoid hatred of Babe Ruth.

Red liked that crazy man and wrote about him unpatronisingly.

And though he was not a snob, he was not a modest man; after all, he was an American – and from The Mid-West to boot.

And perhaps he consciously sculpted his own epitaph when he wrote this about Jimmy Cannon: "At his best, he could make any writer wonder what was the use." Indeed.......

Friday, December 15, 1989

The mirage known as fame

Is there anybody alive who remembers Hall Caine? I am afraid that the question is rhetorical. He was a member of a fast-vanishing breed. He was a novelist and for good measure he was a native of a land about which we hear little.

Did you ever know anybody who came from The Isle of Man?

Well, for better or worse, Hall Caine did.

And you thought that The Isle of Man was all about motor cycling and tax evasion.

Anyhow, the bould Hall wrote novels – and they sold very well.

His work was melodramatic – but he lived in a melodramatic era.

It was so melodramatic that a butcher from Wagga-Wagga in New South Wales pretended that he was the missing heir to a huge estate in England.

He took his case to the courts – and ended up as a guest of Queen Victoria.

And then there was the case of the Sussex shepherd who went missing.

He went missing for so long that people suspected that he was dead.

And eventually a neighbouring shepherd was charged.

And he was found guilty – and he was strung up in Lewes prison until he was very dead. Everybody was happy – except of course the accused man's family and friends.

As Eamonn Kelly would say, things rested so.

Then one fine day the dead man turned up in pub in Sedlescombe.*

That was five years later – the 'dead' shepherd had been in Australia.

Anyhow, you know now why Hall Caine's work is – or was – melodramatic.

Now listen to this sad story.

One morning long ago – actually it was June 13 in 1903 – he was travelling on the train from Liverpool to London.

There was nothing unusual about that, except that in the same carriage a young girl was reading one of his novels.

Of course he was delighted – until the train stopped at Stoke or somewhere thereabouts.

And what did the young girl do?

Would you believe it..... she closed the book ... and yawned.

Too well I know how poor ould Hall felt.

Many is the time I was in a pub or a bus and I died the same death.

I would see a man or a woman or a boy or a girl reading my ould column – and giving up about half way. Now for the almost good news – two nights ago in Mulligan's, of all places, I came very close to fulfilment.

There was this man – obviously a member of the working class, like myself – who was nursing a pint and reading the column.

And when he came to about half-way, he folded the paper into double and hacked on.

And then when he came to the three-quarter way mark, he folded the paper into quadruple.

And while all this was going on, he ignored his pint.

And, believe me, I watched with bated breath, whatever that is.

And I felt that I was on the brink of seeing history made.

For the first time I would see someone reading the column down to the very end.

And what did I do? You will not believe it.

As he came to the last few paragraphs, I lost my nerve.

And I took my glass around to the so-called lounge – and I will never know if history was made.

Journalists are a strange breed – I am not, of course, talking about editors or sub-editors.

I am talking about those like myself and Shane Flynn whose names appear above or below their words.

For them the world is divided into two classes – those who read their pieces and those who don't.

Sometimes, God help us, we get the illusion that we are famous.

I will now tell you how famous I am: I occasionally get letters addressed to 'the other evening paper'.

And I will now tell you a little story which I recall whenever I am tempted to indulge in illusions.

It is set outside Croke Park and the occasion was the All-Ireland Football Final of 1978.

I was in a queue at the Canal end – and a neighbour from down below at home was in front of me. Eventually he took cognisance of my presence – and said: "What are you doing in Dublin?" What could I say?

And I will tell you another story – and it is even more revealing.

Again it is set in Mulligan's, this time in the back room which James Joyce and Peter Roche and myself made famous.

There I was two nights ago having an unquiet drink and chatting up a sweet American girl whom we will call Susan – because that is her name.

And a young man came up to me and said: "I know that you write only about sport. Why don't you ever write about something serious, like politics?"

Only the day before I had written a piece which was partly about politics.

That was in last Tuesday's number of 'Tributaries'.

And for several years before I stumbled into Burgh Quay, I was, more or less, the political correspondent for The Kerryman.

And I will tell you another story which evolved out of that same number of 'Tributaries'.

That was the product of so many hours' work that you wouldn't believe me.

And on Tuesday night a colleague from another publishing house said to me: "That kind of thing doesn't sell papers."

Does anyone know what sells papers? I don't – nor, I suspect, do any of my colleagues in Burgh Quay or elsewhere.

All I know is this: I write what I think – and if it doesn't please or suit some people, that's it.

And I have long believed that the famous man in the Rathmines bus is much brighter than some people believe.

Many is the time someone – usually in a pub – spoke to me about some piece I had written about painting or poetry.

And they spoke knowledgeably and most were people who worked at allegedly humble occupations – such as conducting buses or peeling potatoes or writing in newspapers.

*Sedlescombe is a village in East Sussex; it has two pubs – The Queen's Head and The Coach and Horses.

I should know – I worked there many years ago.

Saturday, March 11, 1989

A change of scenery worked wonders for Hatton's Grace

When we think about The Champion Hurdle – in those intervals when we aren't thinking about The Gold Cup – we tend to forget the first horse that won it for Ireland.

The date had much to do with it: in 1946 racing in Britain was just beginning to pick up after the war.

Eight went down for that first post-Hitler Hurdle; the favourite was a bay gelding named Distel, trained by Maxwell Arnott in Clonsilla in Dublin's north-west suburbs.

He was a smallish handsome horse with three white socks and he had been bred to be a class contender on the flat.

He did fairly well at his intended trade; he won three races and finished third carrying a good lump of weight in The Irish Cesarewitch.

He was then put to hurdling and won seven of his first eight runs; not surprisingly he was entered for the big one.

The cross-channel bookmakers had done their home work; he started at 4/5 even though shorn of the services of his jockey, Mick Gordon, reputedly the only man for whom he would run.

Bobby Ryan deputised for the bould Mick – he was down with a cold; it seemed to make little difference – Distel came up the hill unchallenged and won by four lengths.

Distel was only five and looked set for a long reign but he lost his form and finished well down the field in '47.

The new champion was National Spirit, suitably named for the times – and a very fine horse for good measure.

He won again in '48 – and hurdling seemed to have acquired a flagship; he was still only seven – and could be expected to have at least three more good years.

Racing has, however, an infinite capacity for surprises; when National Spirit cruised home in 1947, not many took much notice of a little horse that finished far behind him in seventh.

Hatton's Grace was already eight, not an age at which a hurdler can be expected to show significant improvement.

He was trained not far from the yard that had sent out Distel – but a change of stable seemed to transform him.

His owners, the well-known Dublin business people Harry and Moya Keogh, decided to send him south to a young trainer who was rapidly making his name.

Vincent O'Brien was then about 30 – and out of a small stable near Doneraile in North Cork he had already landed the Irish Autumn Double.

Those of us who are older remember those exciting days when a genius was essaying his first flights.

Such names as Drybob and Gone and Good Days are like music heard from afar.

And we remember Hatton's Grace too; never did a horse look less the part.

He was small and had a plain head and it was hardly a surprise that on his first appearance in a sales ring he made only 18 guineas.

By the time the Keoghs sent him to Vincent O'Brien, he had won two bumpers and three hurdles out of 23 starts.

It wasn't a bad record – some horses never win a race atall – but neither did it suggest that here was the makings of a champion.

Now listen very carefully: Hatton's Grace had originally been trained by a greatly-respected man – and had done only fairly well. Now read on...

Invariably when the talk turns to Vincent, the story of Hatton's Grace is almost certain to surface.

And you will be told that the amazing transformation was due to Vincent's genius.

That he is a genius is beyond dispute – but in this case the answer may be too facile.

The little horse may have suddenly sprouted wings because he was happier in North Cork than in suburban Dublin.

And possibly it was Aubrey Brabazon who found the key to his treasury of hidden talent.

Aubrey was to be his partner in his second life; they seemed to get on as well as steak and fried potatoes.

Hatton's Grace expanded in Churchtown like an Irishman who goes to London and finds himself.

It is an amazing fact that after only two races out of O'Brien's yard the little horse won The Champion Hurdle.

Needless to say, on that famous day in 1949 National Spirit was a roaring-and-shouting favourite. In a field of 14 he started at 5/4.

His regular pilot, Ron Smyth, had retired – but his new partner, Bryan

Marshall, was no daw; in fact he was deemed the best of his generation.

There was nothing dramatic about the first of the two miles – then at the half-way mark came the start of a sensation.

Hatton's Grace exploded out of the pack and went three lengths clear – the posse never got near him. National Spirit came in a distant fourth.

All Britain – and especially England – went into mourning.

That was the start of the British-Irish festival rivalry that now threatens to outrun Coronation Street.

Of course excuses abounded. National Spirit hadn't been himself; he had fallen at Plumpton a few months previously and hadn't got back his confidence.

So the story went. Then came next year, as is usually the case.

National Spirit ran like his old self and led as they came to the final flight.

Then the bould Aubrey gave his little friend the message: Hatton's Grace and National Spirit came to the hurdle together, the English horse blundered – the race was over.

The two champions met again in 1951. Their presence kept the field down to eight.

You will be amazed to hear that neither was favourite – that dubious honour went to a rising star, the unbeaten Average.

It was a difficult occasion for Aubrey Brabazon; he had been retained to ride the favourite; of course being Aubrey he honoured his word.

Tim Molony got the leg up on the little hero; an almighty crowd came to see the shoot-out between the dual champions and Average.

At the half-way mark the little Irish horse looked out of contention.

He gradually made up ground – but National Spirit was two lengths clear as they came to the last.

Once again the big English horse blundered; Tim Molony's ride up the hill was like a lap of honour.

National Spirit and Hatton's Grace went to the post again in 1952 – both were unplaced; a new star was in the firmament; Sir Ken won the first leg of his hat-trick.

The Keoghs's little horse will always be a folk hero to my generation.

I was a serious punter in those days – and my maxim was: "Leave it to Mr. O'Brien."

Friday, October 29, 1993

Marathon running is child's play!

On Wednesday we wrote about the marathon and its remarkable tailpiece – the running of several hundred children along the footpath by Stephen's Green.

It was a wondrous sight: some of those indulging their fantasies were hardly five; the little girls were just as enthusiastic as the boys.

It reminded me of an event which happened early this year, a truly amazing event which got very little publicity.

It involved thousands of children who set out on foot from Sudan; their ambition was to reach Kenya – they saw no future for them in their wartorn and half-starving country.

Journalists who witnessed the exodus failed to discover how it originated; they questioned several of the children and all gave much the same answer – "Everybody was walking – and so I walked too."

What intrigued the journalists was the children's high degree of organisation: some were deputed to gather firewood, others to collect water, others to do the cooking – when there was something to cook.

This epic march went on for months; I do not know where those heroic children are now – they are probably in a refugee camp.

Let us return to the juvenile stampede on Monday. Who organised it? Did it just happen? I said on Wednesday that perhaps it happened in my imagination. Will somebody confirm my story?

As I watched that innocent children's crusade, I was reminded of another kind of running, a sight familiar to all who love rivers and their denizens.

About half a mile beyond Castle Island on the road to Abbeyfeale there is a great vantage point whence to watch the running of fish.

When the autumn floods come, you can see the fish running up along the concrete floor under Clounagh Bridge.

The mature fish are going up to the spawning beds; tiny fish, some hardly fingerlings, go with them – they are caught up in the madness, or in the sanity, of the running.

Many of those juvenile trout are unable to negotiate that concrete floor; the current defeats them and they are washed out to the calmer water on the sides, water so shallow that their tiny bodies are half exposed.

When they have rested for a while, they try again; some manage to get beyond the concrete floor; most are again washed to the sides – but they try and try again.

Their persistence is wonderful to behold; Bruce's spider wouldn't tie their laces.

Why do those little fish run with their elders? I am not a scientist – I doubt if the scientists know.

Trout live in communities; perhaps the little trout feel lonely when the elders start to run – I don't know. All I can say is that it is all enthralling.

Let us return to the Dublin marathon; there are those amongst us who have long been forecasting its demise.

Some years ago there was almost a consensus that The Grand National was doomed; I was in the minority – I was utterly confident that it would survive; I said so and wrote so.

The great Aintree race is as much a part of English life as roast beef and cottage cheese and weak beer and football pools and The Changing of The Guard and bottled sauce and fish-and-chips and toast-and-marmalade – the gates of pessimism cannot prevail against it.

The Dublin Marathon is hardly comparable but it has become part of our lives; we would miss it.

On Monday I had planned to be in Clanbrassil Street to watch the elite come around first time; I miscalculated and was about a minute late.

All wasn't lost: there I met Frank Greally and got all the information.

Frank at this stage was fairly confident that John Treacy would prevail; believe it or not, I was mildly disappointed – as an unrepentant son of Kerry I was batting for John Griffin.

Of course I didn't begrudge John his victory; he deserved it – and he needed it. I will attempt to explain.

Aficionados of athletics needed no convincing of his greatness; the generality did.

He won the World Cross-Country Championship twice; he won a marathon in Los Angeles; he took a silver medal in the marathon in the Californian Olympics – and yet the generality here at home had their doubts.

They tended to judge him on the Barcelona Olympics; that marathon was a disaster for John.

He had prepared as thoroughly as a human can; he was ready to attack his Everest.

And the conditions came right for him: it rained on Saturday night; there was a fresh breeze on the Sunday; the temperature was well below the average for that time of year by the Mediterranean.

And yet it all went horribly wrong; it was the worst day in John's career; after only a few miles he knew that he had nothing to give.

Mentally and physically he was as near to perfection as a human could be – and yet it all went wrong.

On Monday he prevailed.

Wednesday, February 2, 1994.

Stoking up a fond memory

Very soon in this paper I hope to divulge the findings of a survey that was long overdue in the context of the island of Ireland. Now read on ...

Why are so many people in this island so passionately devoted to clubs in the other island?

And while I am at it, I might as well tell you about the club in my cupboard.

In mainstream football I "follow" Manchester Untied; I rejoiced like a little boy on that night a few years ago in Rotterdam when they took the European Cup Winners' Cup.

Liverpool are next in my affections; Arsenal come third; I must admit that they were equal first with Untied when seven Irishmen were regulars at Highbury.

And I didn't fully understand the nature of mixed emotions until that crazy afternoon at Wembley when United got a brace of equalising goals five minutes from full time – and lost out to Liam Brady's genius.

The club in my cupboard are Stoke City. And the source of my affection goes back a long time.

It began with Arnold Bennett; there's many a point gone over the bar and many a pint gone down the red lane since first I read The Grim Smile Of The Five Towns.

Bennett made the mistake of becoming popular in his lifetime; almost inevitably his reputation has suffered; it hardly bothers him.

If you chance to read his best story, The Death Of Simon Fuge, you will appreciate how fine an artist he could be when he wasn't boiling the pot.

My memories of Stoke were reactivated on Monday night.

I was sitting in my usual neutral corner in Cassidy's of Camden Street watching that enthralling game between Bolton Wanderers and Arsenal; now for the second time today, read on . . .

I was still in the afterglow of Owen Coyle's great goal when two innocent bysitters got up and joined me.

Seamus Brennan is well known as a principal player in Viking Travel in Thomas Street; his friend on Monday night is well known too – he is paid to mind us when we are asleep and when we are awake.

When the statutory exchanges had been completed, Seamus said: "Do you know that Tony Waddington died on Saturday?"

And thus the three of us fell – or perhaps rose – into talking about Stoke-on-Trent and its long-suffering football club.

Tony Waddington's name may mean little to the young generation; you could argue that he was one of the greatest managers ever to have graced English football.

While he was on the bridge at Stoke City, romance was alive and very well; Arnold Bennett would have been proud.

When he came to The Victoria Ground, the old club in the heart of The Potteries was sinking silently into The Third Division.

That was in the season of 1961-62. Waddington quickly showed his hand – and his heart was in it; he ransomed Stanley Matthews from Blackpool.

The magic raider of the right wing was then 46; obviously his manager at Blackpool deemed him no more than a name player – he was let go for a few thousand pounds.

Who said "They never come back"? Robin Hood came back; Jesse James came back; Stanley Matthews most certainly came back.

Many of Stoke's followers believed that Waddington's bold venture owed more to romanticism than judgement; Matthews had been fourteen years away and had almost disappeared from the public mind.

The maestro was revitalised by the grim smile of the five towns; Stoke prospered – and ended the season well up the table.

And, of course, the presence of Matthews caused the turnstiles to make music.

Waddington now had a little cash; he bought some outstanding players; Matthews found himself playing alongside Dennis Viollet and Jimmy McIlroy.

Stoke won the Second Division championship in the season of 1962-'63 Believe it or not, Matthews scored the goal that clinched the title; this was Roy Of The Rovers at its most outrageous.

It wasn't to be roses all the way; Stoke struggled.

Gradually Waddington reinforced his expedition; by the dawn of the seventies he had assembled what was surely Stoke's best-ever team.

It included Gordon Banks; Leicester City had offloaded him when they acquired a young lad called Peter Shilton.

And in the season of 1971-'72 Stoke won their first major trophy in the 110 years of the club's existence.

I was at a rugby international game at Lansdowne Road on the greatest day in Tony Waddington's career as a manager – part of my mind was at Wembley.

Stoke beat Chelsea 2-1 in the final of The League Cup; Terry Conroy scored the first and helped Geroge Eastham to score the other.

The presence of those two purists symbolised Waddington's concept of football.

Stoke now had a few pounds in their biscuit tin; Jimmy Greenhoff and Alan Hudson were brought to The Victoria Ground.

And in the season of 1974-'75 it seemed that The Potters were poised to achieve what a decade before would have seemed unthinkable.

Stoke were the bookies' favourites for about half the season; then a plague of injuries far beyond the national average smote them – they finished fifth.

That was to be The Potters' peak; Waddington disagreed with the directors over the sale of players – demoralisation set in; I had ringside evidence.

I was on the The South Terrace at Highbury one Saturday when Stoke played Arsenal in The League - "played" wasn't the word.

Tony Waddington quit in the spring of 1977; Stoke went down.

The great romantic went to Crewe Alexandra with whom he had spent most of his career as a player.

He had survived the Normandy landing; Crewe proved beyond him – after two barren seasons there he drifted out of football.

He spent his late years in that town at the heart of Britain's rail web; he passed away at the age of seventy.

Friday, March 24, 1995

Cheltenham revisited

On the plane to Birmingham on the Tuesday morning of last week a sweet-faced hostess introduced herself to me: "My name is Breda. I think you know Paddy Freeman . . ." Indeed I do. Who doesn't know the original Ginger Man . . .

I was relieved to hear that he was fit and well and up and running; he hasn't been seen in his old haunts for ages.

Rumours abounded; Paddy is as intimate with the world of gambling as Lester Piggott is with the ups and downs of Epsom racetrack – it was being whispered that he had been employed by The Football Association to help untangle the alleged match-fixing conspiracy.

Perhaps it is true; anyhow, we hope to see him back soon in Mulligan's – politically correct or not.

In the little station bar in Cheltenham Spa I missed the small man with his white hair combed into a fringe; I have no doubt that he was – and hopefully still is – an authority on the growing of leeks.

Missing also were the two dear little ladies with their red-ribboned straw hats; I hope that we will see them back; the bar was in the hands of a pleasant young man who spoke with the cider-apple accent of his native heath.

Across the road there was little change: The Midland, the pub nearest to the station, has long been familiar to Irish racegoers.

For years it was about the scruffiest tavern in the west of England or in the west of anywhere; now it has been slightly refurbished but remains as homely as ever.

A glowing coalfire greets the traveller; you can get an excellent pint of Stella Artois for £1.60.

They (whoever 'they' are) say that if you stand for five minutes on O'Connell Bridge or in Charing Cross Road or anywhere in Manhattan, you will meet somebody you know: if you spend five minutes in The Midland on an evening after racing, you will meet too many.

One day long ago I decided to see what The Midland is like when not populated with racegoers. And so I went down from Birmingham on an early train and found that homely pub crowded.

Most of its denizens were in their working clothes and many were railway men; I had almost forgotten that Cheltenham Spa is a major junction.

Thence you can voyage to the extremes of the south-west or away to Fishguard or over to London and beyond or, unless you have more sense, up to the north-east of Scotland.

Two doors from The Midland there is a Tote betting shop; I know local men who have never been out to Prestbury Park; they watch on television – and, of course, every decent pub has a runner to take the bets and bring back the money.

I know a grand man from Dublin who has lived for about forty years near Cheltenham; he watches the festival in The Midland but with a difference – he dresses as if for the races.

The turf – and especially the world of hurdling and chasing – continues to abound in stories.

The amazing progress of Alderbrook from the flat to the hurdles is an obvious example.

When he was sent to Kim Bailey, only about two months remained before Cheltenham: Alderbrook was and is a very smart horse on the flat, a winner at such prestigious tracks as Goodwood and Longchamp – but hurdling is a different race game.

The trainer thought that he had been given an impossible brief: The Champion Hurdle is not for novices.

Some horses take slowly and reluctantly to the hurdles; some do not take atall; some take as readily as seagulls to the slipstream of the plough – Alderbrook was such an apprentice.

In the race at Wincanton which we spoke about a few days ago he was having only his second trip over hurdles; he ran and skipped with the zest of a novice and the expertise of a veteran.

I was mightily impressed; so were those connoisseurs of reality, the bookmakers; his price for The Champion Hurdle had been a derisory 50/1 – next morning it was 42 points less.

Alderbrook's rise was liberally etched with romance; the ascent of his partner at Cheltenham, a young man named Norman Williamson, would make Nat Gould's highest flights of fancy seem prosaic.

Until the day of The Champion Hurdle he had never ridden a winner at The Festival; by Thursday afternoon he had landed the big double of hurdle and chase and piloted two other winners for great measure.

And he had proven that our poor backward little island hasn't lost its faculty for producing brilliant riders.

We down in my part of Kerry will look on Norman as one of our own: he comes from near Mallow; we are so intimately acquainted with North-West Cork that we regard it as part of our spiritual territory – we thought nothing of cycling to Mallow Races in leaner times.

He is a graduate from the point-to-points, a dura matrix, a hard school.

In his Irish incarnation he worked for a trainer in East Limerick, a guru who was famous as just about the shrewdest judge of horses and men in the business – now read on . . .

One day at a point-to-point the young Corkman came to grief on a hotly-fancied mount from the stable and broke an arm in the process; worse was to follow – the famous judge of horses and men told him not to come back.

Jonjo O'Neill had a similar experience in his green youth: while working in a stable at The Curragh, he was involved in a fall; it cost the horse his life and Jonjo his job.

It isn't only prophets that aren't recognised in their own land.

Success is a great elixir: horses are extremely sensitive; if you have confidence, it rubs off on them.

Norman Williamson went to Uttoxeter on Saturday; there he got a leg up on a horse called Lucky Lane in The Midland Grand National; his mount had no great form and at twelve years of age was unlikely to improve; Norman adopted bold tactics and brought him home at twelve to one.

And Michael Hourigan followed up his great victory with Dorans Pride: at Limerick on Saturday he saddled three winners – King's Cherry and Lisaleen River and Queen Of The Lakes. It was a good week for The Deep South.

Sunday World, September 1, 1996

Hoary myth is dead

I wasn't in Dublin on the eve of Clontarf and I haven't the slightest inkling of the mood on that day; perhaps the atmosphere was little different from the usual.

Perhaps the fishermen down below in Ringsend were following the ancient profession adorned by Peter and his brethren and perhaps Molly's ancestors were busier than usual because a day of abstinence was imminent – all I know is that the peasants of Brabant milked their cows on the morning of Waterloo.

I suppose it is fair to say that this afternoon's showdown is awaited as eagerly as any hurling All-Ireland ever; it isn't too long since you could stroll up to Croke Park after the pubs closed and be sure of getting in to one terrace or the other.

The attendance at the final between Galway and Kilkenny in 1975 was under 54,000. Whence has come the revolution, if it is really a revolution?

The underlying cause may be simple; in the last quarter of a century we have seen a hoary myth shattered beyond repair. All the mumblings of the traditionalists cannot put it together again but of course we still have to suffer the old husbands' tales about how great the game was long ago.

I am old enough to remember when the keeper was fair (foul) game for the hitmen and when the famous dust rising from the goalmouths in Thurles didn't always come from strokes aimed at the sliotar.

The good old days are here now. The old husbands will tell you that such arts as the double are no more. Gerald McCarthy seems assured of his place in folklore as its last great exponent.

The extra velocity of the new ball has made the double much more difficult to achieve. It has also of course changed the tactics of the game: most keepers now can drop the puck-out to within 40 yards of goal – indeed with the help of the wind they can trouble their counterparts.

I need hardly add that we have seen great hurling in The Leinster and Munster championships this season. At least six games have whetted the appetites – and the semi-finals did nothing to unwhet them.

Galway and Wexford produced a splendid game. Limerick fell below expectations but to me it seemed that for the first time in their history we saw Antrim progress from being pretenders to becoming contenders.

The long absence of Limerick and Wexford from the crock of gold under the rainbow has added to the ferment.

A fair proportion of the lads and lassies whose hearts will rise and sink and rise this afternoon have never known their counties win September glory.

To me it seems only a few years ago since Limerick took gold – in fact, 23 years have gone by; Wexford haven't been in the winners' enclosure since 1968.

The people who will most create the atmosphere today are not the players or the younger followers but the veteran aficionados, men and women who have suffered so many false springs and so many broken harvests – they are not so much hungry as ravenous.

They yearn to walk down Fitzgibbon Street like a conquering army. I should be more excited about today's game than about any hurling final ever because both forces are dear to my heart. I need hardly add that in our part of Kerry we follow the Green-and-White.

Indeed there were times when I grieved for Limerick more than for Kerry because I was confident that our absence from Croke Park would be short. Alas...

I grieved especially after the All-Ireland simi-final between Galway and Limerick in 1981. That was the occasion when Sean Foley was very harshly sent off.

Sean wrote me a long letter about his trauma: he felt that his dismissal had cost Limerick the game and probably the All-Ireland. I never showed that letter to anybody – Sean's sorrow was intensely private.

Limerick folk will tell you that the tragic loss of that semi-final cast a gloom from which it has taken a long time to recover.

My admiration for the hurlers of Wexford and their followers is hardly a secret: on their great days they seem to elevate the ancient craft onto a new plateau.

I am thinking especially about the Leinster final of 1976. On that astonishing occasion they devastated Kilkenny with an art that seemed to have been invented by the Black-and-Amber; we saw points flying home like arrows from the bow of William Tell.

If asked to name my favourite person in Irish sport, Tony Doran would be a warm contender: he had a quality that was hard to define but easy to recognise. I will content myself by describing that quality as heroic.

He always seemed to be striving to go beyond his limits; the spirit seemed as important as his range of skills.

When I invoke the term "heroic", I think of Mick Mackey and Tom Cheasty and Pat Hartigan and George O'Connor. You may wonder why I didn't mention Ring: Christy achieved his great deeds by his superb skills.

The maestro from Cloyne rarely did anything that surprised you but he did the fundamental things so well that he was very hard to counter.

The heroic isn't altogether past tense: Mick Houlihan and Ciaran Carey have a touch of it – so has Martin Storey. They could be the stars of this enthralling battle but the gods have a tendency to write disquieting scenarios.

Thus sometimes the bit players shine while the stars are dimmed. I must confess that there was a showdown in hurling to which I looked forward with even greater anticipation than I do to that of this afternoon.

It was arranged for a Sunday afternoon in the 1860s and I was twelve years of age. Lovers of Charles Kickham and his great book Knocknagow need no telling. The teams were to be the farmers and the farmers' boys. It threatened to be class warfare.

The game wasn't all ticket but there was a great crowd in The Field. Twenty-one good men and true would do battle for their tribes.

Mat Donovan, I need hardly add, was captain of the labourers. "There was a hush and an anxious look on many a face as he strode towards the middle of the field" and "Some of the players were quite pale and their teeth were chattering with excitement".

Mat is puzzled when he sees that the opposition are not taking their places. The explanation is soon forthcoming: their captain, Tom Cuddehy, is missing.

A young lad comes running and says "Ould Paddy Loughlan's daughter is after running away with him". The farmers wouldn't play without him and so it is agreed to play a mixed match.

I never forgave Paddy Loughlan's daughter – she almost turned me against the feminine gender for life. It is most unlikely that some oul lad's daughter will run off with Ciaran Carey or Martin Storey before the throw-in this afternoon.

The captains, incidentally, were rather more important in the old days. Sometimes they acted as dual referees. Could you imagine that happening now...

By this morning every aspect of every player involved this afternoon has been parsed and analysed and all the anticipated duels have been scrutinised. The truth of course is that many of these duels never materialise.

Hurling, far more that Gaelic football or soccer or rugby, is tantalisingly unpredictable. When I make a forecast about the outcome of a game in those three, I have comparatively solid reasons.

When you make a prediction about a hurling game in which the teams seem to be evenly matched, you are whistling past your obituary as a pundit.

To argue that hurling is akin to cricket may seem a wild statement – but think about it...

The ball in both is about the same size; at times they can travel at about a hundred miles an hour and can behave wickedly both in the air and off the pitch.

In the context of Gaelic football and soccer and rugby you are often dealing with inches; in hurling and cricket you are sometimes dealing in centimetres.

A tiny edge off the bat can cost a wicket; a similar edge off the caman can make or save a goal.

Sometimes I suspect that the gremlins reserve their most insidious tricks for All-Ireland hurling finals and they never seem to have any difficulty getting tickets.

They seem to take an especial delight in tormenting keepers. When I saw Michael Walsh giving away a goal in an All-Ireland final, I knew then that no keeper was invulnerable.

Joe Quaid and Damien Fitzhenry have been in splendid form all season. Limerick's keeper may seem to have an advantage because he has already played in a final but his counterpart is more familiar with Croke Park.

Those Wexford people who believe in omens may take heart from the fact that Liam Griffin owns a string of hotels; so does Brian McEniff who led Donegal in their year of glory.

How can I make a forecast? My heart says Limerick. My head says Wexford. My head is in confusion. I have seen Limerick only once this season, that is apart from television. I have seen Wexford three times – they excelled against Offaly and Galway.

I have no doubts about Limerick's defenders and midfielders. Unless their forwards make a great leap upward, my neighbours in the hills north of Castle Island will not see the glow from the bonfires in Abbeyfeale and Broadford and Templeglantine and Castlemahon and beyond.

I need hardly add that the hoary myth is the belief that Cork, Tipperary and Kilkenny are hurling's aristocrats.

Friday, December 8, 1989

Las Vegas in a field near Clondalkin

Now it can be told: about 20 years ago I was invited to a travellers' wedding, one of the few infidels ever to enjoy the privilege. There was no mystery about the invitation: I had been their ombudsman and amanuensis for a good many years.

The ombudsman part consisted mainly in pleading for leniency from local farmers who didn't look too kindly on having their gates lifted from the hinges so that travellers' horses could enjoy a night of illicit grass.

As amanuensis I had to deal mainly with The Department of Social Welfare and a certain Hector Grey.

Anyhow, it was a splendid wedding; the singing was especially great; if you have ever heard Margaret Barry, you will appreciate the passion which the travelling people bring to their songs.

Since I came to Dublin, I have more or less lost touch with the travellers; if I meet any of them, it is usually in mid-December – some of my old neighbours come up to sell holly and Christmas trees.

And so I knew nothing about a remarkable event which took place last week – until it was all over.

Jim Byrne, God rest him, for many years mine host of The Hideout in Kilcullen and the most inventive publican that ever pulled a pint, would have relished the aforementioned event.

Once upon a time he planned to stage a 'repeat' of the famous Donnelly-Cooper fight – in, of course, Donnelly's Hollow.

It was to be the highlight of a local pageant – but, for a variety of reasons, it fell through.

Anyhow, it wouldn't have been 'for real' but a fight that took place last week in a field near Clondalkin most certainly was.

The protagonists were two young men of the traveller tribe; the fight, far from being impromptu, was well organised.

I do not know if there was a ring; I know that it was a bare-knuckle fight.

And that brought a whiff of the nineteenth century, of the great days when Mace and Gully and Sayers and their fellows enjoyed the prestige reserved for professional footballers now.

William Hazlitt should have been in that field near Clondalkin last week; Pierce Egan too would have been enthralled.

There was a crowd of about 500 to watch the two young pugilists – and of course some busybody alerted the gardai.

They came but could do nothing. How could they when they had to deal with a frenzy of women and children...

The fight ran its course. Eventually the gardai carted the two combatants off to hospital; they were treated for cuts and bruises and went back to the bosoms of their families.

What a pity that someone wasn't perched up in a tree with a movie camera – it would have made great television.

Another source of great television also went waste last week.

This was not in a field near Clondalkin but on a mountainside in Wales

The protagonists were the local foresters and about 500 wild goats.

Goats, as we all know, have an extremely catholic taste in food; they may not eat everything in sight but go as near as makes little difference.

And seemingly the goats on the slopes of Snowdon do no good for the trees.

And so one day last week the foresters assembled in considerable numbers and set out to round up the nannies and the billies.

They were armed with what seemed a foolproof plan: the goats would be funnelled into a gulley where a net would do the rest.

And then the goats would be transported up to a part of the Highlands where there are no trees to damage – we were not told what the good people of Scotland did to deserve all this.

Anyhow, the bould foresters set to work armed with two-way radios: the goats would have to fight bare-handed.

The head of the party issued a remarkable rallying cry a few moments before the kick-off: "If a billy goat comes at you, just shout at him – and he will stop."

The good man may know a great deal about trees but his knowledge of goats seems to be rather sketchy – as some of his round-up party found out to their cost.

The score at the end of a long and arduous day was: Injured Foresters 17, Captured Goats 0.

As night began to descend, the goats were high up on the top of a disused slate quarry whither no human could pursue them – and they were laughing their heads and their horns off.

The head forester is alleged to have said that they should be shot – he seems to be a bad loser.

My guess is that there will be a replay – watch this space.

It all reminds me of a famous story which I have told here before.

It is set in Paris about 20 years ago and is absolutely authentic. The protagonists were the local pigeons – thousands and thousands of them – and the city fathers.

The latter were under ever-increasing pressure from local spoilsports who objected to the pigeons' penchant for aerial bombardment.

And so one Monday morning they scattered grain all around the fair city, grain that was dressed with sleeping powder.

And that evening the dozy pigeons – thousands and thousands of them – were transported over to The Vosges in unmarked vans. The spoilsports were happy – until about three o'clock on the Thursday afternoon.

The sky began to darken over Monmartre and The Madeleine and The Arc de Triomphe, not to mention The Rue Haussmann and The Opera and The Place de Carousel – the pigeons were back.

Friday, January 5, 1990

Aficion, a mix of love, expertise

There is, after all, a time machine, even if it owes nothing to technology, modern or otherwise. And about four o'clock last Sunday it ferried me back over a great many years.

I was in Flanagan's, that landmark in Harold's Cross, having a few not-so-quiet drinks with three alarmingly articulate friends – and then it happened.

The warriors who had battled for Cork City against St. Patrick's Athletic came in – and suddenly I was back to the days when I played rugby for Castle Island.

My young self was there amongst them, mulling over the game that had just ended, having fantasies about what might have been.

City, you see, had just been beaten by a late late goal that had come like a streak of lightning out of a clear blue sky.

It's all very well talking about positive thinking – but there are times when I feel that the concept should be sent back to the cosy pages of Reader's Digest.

That, I suppose, is rather unfair; there is a great need for positive thinking but you can overdo it.

And when you have just been rather unluckily defeated – whether in soccer or rugby or hurling or love or whatever – you would be astonishingly mature if you didn't indulge in what might have been.

And mature people, astonishingly so or otherwise, do not play games; sport is the last refuge of the immature.

And the faces of those young men in Flanagan's told their own tale.

It may sound ludicrous and indeed unbelievable to people in the real world outside – but defeat even in a little match can make you feel that the sun will never rise again.

I am well aware that Frank Haffey sang in the bath after England had beaten Scotland 10-3 – and, in case you didn't know, he was the goalkeeper.

Frank used to say: "I make a living out of football but I don't let it get me down."

Later he repented – and the awfulness of the day in Wembley smote him.

And he banished himself to the Antipodes; no doubt he would have gone further if there had been further to go.

Let us return to Flanagan's last Sunday evening; that meeting of Patrick's and City had not been a little game – far from it.

The points were precious to both: Patrick's are hungering and thirsting for the championship; City are hovering worriedly above the relegation zone.

The championship pennant hasn't come to Inchicore since those golden days when Shay Gibbons was Patrick's spearhead; the good people of the environ would dearly love to see it flying over Richmond Park.

And relegation . . . there's the rub. For those immediately involved, it is like a death in the family.

And there is more to it than the fusion of guilt and humiliation.

There is the cut in the wages. And there is the disincentive of playing before smaller crowds.

And, paradoxical though it may seem, there is the tougher opposition.

Proverbially it is tough at the top; a strange fact of football life is that it is tougher at the bottom.

Down there you meet the ambitious youngsters hungering to ascend and the veterans grimly determined to cling to their profession.

I do not expect that Cork City will go down – but a slide can prove agonisingly hard to correct.

I watched last Sunday's game in excellent company.

By chance I met John MacNamara, a man as devoted to Cork City as that famous cat was to Dick Whittington. And he told me a revealing fact about soccer in the United States. It is played mostly in the schools attended by the poor – because their parents cannot afford the gear necessary for the gridiron game.

John should know: he used to referee schools football in New England.

And his knowledge of the game would flummox Jimmy Hill, not to mention Jimmy Greaves and Ian St. John.

And on Sunday he made a curious little bit of history – you will find it hard to believe.

After about 25 minutes' play he dipped into a deep pocket and produced a hip flask.

I couldn't have been more astonished if he'd produced a Colt 45 or even a Colt 38.

The hip flask, as every dog and cat in the streets and in the fields and in the woods well know, belongs in the better seats in the stands at rugby internationals.

And it is mainly worn by those who wouldn't know a prop from a post.

John, however, has an excuse: his pewter flask was given to him about ten years ago by his brother Jim.

On Sunday morning he filled it for the first time – in, I think, The Punchbowl.

And of course on Sunday afternoon he emptied it for the first time, not altogether on his own it must be admitted.

We were joined in Flanagan's by two other aficionados: Christy Looney is vice-chairman of Cork City; Jimmy Edwards used to be a post office sorter – for good measure, he is devoted to St. Patrick's.

With us there was an American girl who had just witnessed her first soccer game; now she was hearing he first post-match analysis.

And for about an hour and a half it seemed as if nothing else but football mattered in this mortal world.

Then John and Christy departed for The Deep South – and Jimmy prepared for a stint as Master of Ceremonies and resident singer in Clarke's of Wexford Street.

It was a good day: I greatly respect people who go into the arena and seek glory while risking humiliation.

———

Wednesday, February 14, 1990

Drama In Tokyo

Seldom has a sporting event had so quiet a prelude and so tumultuous an aftermath; last week the imminent fight in Tokyo was hardly mentioned in the pubs; on Sunday night there was talk of little else.

If I got a ten-penny piece for every time I was asked "What did you think of the fight?", I could afford to achieve a long-time ambition – to have a real Irish breakfast in The Shelbourne some day.

My verdict, for what it's worth, is that James Douglas won, as the saying goes, "fair and square."

I watched the fight on television on Sunday morning and on video in The Goalpost on the way back from Croke Park – and am convinced that Douglas could have been up before ten if the referee had taken up the count correctly.

If you watch the video again, you will see that Douglas while on the canvas looked very aware, got up with no great difficulty, and came out and boxed brilliantly over the next two rounds.

That is one aspect; more important is the long-established dictum – "The referee's decision shall be final." Even Don King, the great campaigner for truth and justice, cannot get around that.

The other long count, the oft-discussed interval in the Gene Tunney-Jack Dempsey fight in 1927, shouldn't be such a source of controversy as it has been – the film shows clearly that Tunney could easily have got up before a correct ten.

Several accounts described the result of the Tokyo fight as the most sensational in the history of the heavyweight championship; I feel that they exaggerated.

Those of us who are older remember how little chance James Braddock was given when he went in as a substitute against Max Baer; he won handsomely on points.

And have we all forgotten about the first meeting of the youthful Cassius Clay and "unbeatable" Sonny Liston . . .

You could back the boy from Louisville at 10/1; I had a few pounds on him, mainly because Old Moore (Archie, not the man of the almanac) said he would win.

So much did the experts under-rate Douglas that several leading boxing writers didn't bother to travel to Japan – but at least one journalist got the result right.

His name is Tim May; he works on a paper called *The Columbus Despatch* – Columbus, Ohio, is the new champion's home town.

The fight produced a few nice one-liners. Don King, of course, got into the act: "Truth should prevail." Indeed . . .

The fight game suddenly seems to be imbued with philosophy and religion.

Listen to what Trevor Berbick, Tyson's chief sparring partner, had to say: "God is not sleeping and justice must prevail."

Douglas said: "I did it all for Jesus Christ."

No doubt he was serious – and worse things have been done in His name.

Now in hindsight we can all see that Douglas had a fairly impressive record: he won 30 of his 36 professional fights; he lost four and drew one – the odd fight was declared a no-contest.

For good measure he was Olympic champion.

His prestige would have been much higher but for his disastrous showing against Tony Tucker in 1987.

James Douglas, incidentally, set out to make his living at a different sport – and discovered the truth of an American dictum: "The ultimate in frustration is being a six foot three basketball player."

Friday, May 12, 1989

Walking tall in the garden

Yesterday I saw Brooklyn Bridge for the first time; it didn't look its best in the grey downpour – nevertheless, it was easy to appreciate the boldness that conceived it and the skill that brought it about.

New York is like a living museum of engineering; even the ancient Romans would have to give it the nod, especially in the long narrow island called Manhattan where the laws of physics have been tested to their utmost.

This famous bridge joins Brooklyn and Lower Manhattan and has evoked more writing than any other link in the world – and I am not forgetting The Coathanger in Sydney.

Hart Crane, the tragic poet from Ohio, lived for a while in Brooklyn and devoted an epic to the bridge. He was obsessed with water – and at an early age was drowned when he jumped off a ship between Havana and New York.

Bridges are beautiful things, even the humblest; they are a symbol of man's capacity for creativity.

It isn't too difficult to guess at their origin: millions of years ago one of our forefathers saw a tree fallen across a river – and said to himself: "What the wind can do, so can I."

It isn't so easy to guess at the origin of golf; I have heard a wild array of theories about it.

The most common and the most plausible is that it originated among the shepherds of Scotland. One day Hamish was stroking a round pebble with his crooked stick; it went into a hole – and, lo, one of the world's great games was born.

Basketball, we are told, evolved in the mid-west of the United States; it was played in the barns and shortened the long winters – but of the genius who first thought of aiming a ball at a basket we have no record.

The seed he put down has produced a mighty harvest; basketball is now probably the most popular game in the United States, at least in terms of the numbers playing.

The reasons for its popularity aren't hard to divine; you don't require great talent to enjoy playing it – and, more important, it must be the safest of all games. A few nights ago I saw a professional game in which two players wore spectacles.

American Football, like Rugby, is a highly dangerous game; I understand why so many parents encourage their children to take up basketball.

The catch, of course, is that unless you reach an altitude of over six and a half feet, you are unlikely to make the top grade.

John Updike has written a short story about this dilemma; the anti-hero has all the skills but he is only six foot three – and he experiences the ultimate in frustration.

Basketball is so big here now that it has more or less ousted boxing from Madison Square Garden. Of course television was a factor too in the diminishing of The Garden as a boxing centre. Viewing time is the name of the game now – that was why Muhammad Ali and George Foreman stepped into a ring away down below in Zaire at some crazy hour when they should have been in bed.

Nevertheless, it comes as a mild shock to discover that The Garden is now more intimately associated with Rod Strickland than with Mike Tyson; Rod is a star with New York Knickerbockers – The Garden is their home.

There last Tuesday night the home team played Chicago Bulls. I am far from being an expert on basketball but even I could see that this was a game of the highest quality.

Both squads were composed almost entirely of brown pine trees and seemingly the stars are getting taller by the generation.

Michael Jordan is one of the brightest stars in the game today. He plays with Chicago Bulls; his forte is attack. The papers raved about him on Wednesday morning.

Indeed, the analysis – as distinct from the report – in the New York Times was so obsessed with him that it mentioned only four other players. One of those was Sidney Green who had the dubious distinction of committing the foul on Jordan that swung the game for Chicago.

At the end of normal time the teams were level at 103 points each. The Knicks – as, of course, they are called – had contained Jordan fairly well in the four periods of normal time.

However, in the extra period he cut loose and scored nine points. The Bulls won 120 to 109. He got two great scores but the highlight of his display was a pass he made in normal time. We would say that it was made on the blind; the American call it a no-look pass – anyhow, it homed in sweetly to a team-mate about thirty feet away.

In the bar after the game the fans spoke of nobody but Jordan. Seemingly the home coach had made ingenious plans to frustrate him - they worked well enough until extra time. As I have said, the report in The Times mentioned only four other players.

I must concede, however, that the piece had its good points: for instance, where we would say a player levelled the score, reporter Sam Goldaper said 'he deadlocked'. I like it.

And yesterday also in the realm of sport I came upon a new usage. A baseball game was abandoned owing to the rain and we were told that the date for the make-up hadn't been fixed.

So now you know that 'make-up' refers to more than lovers' quarrels.

And while all this was going on, the search continued for the missing baseball player Rick Leach whom I mentioned yesterday. You remember that he disappeared shortly before his team, the Texas Rangers, set out from a Manhattan hotel to play the tenants at Yankee Stadium.

Leach obviously had difficulty in hiding; before he became a professional baseball player, he was a famous quarter back; he is 32 and his face is well known. Obviously the police got a tip-off. They found him in a little hotel in mid-Manhattan. And seemingly they knew something. They searched his room and discovered a quantity of marijuana.

Now he is in trouble both with the law and his club.

We are told that he is being held for 'medical evaluation'.

Leach is quoted as saying: "I'm a man and I stand up to what is coming to me."

They are fine words but I wouldn't care to be in his shoes.

If you did something like that down at home long ago, it would take you a very long time to live it down – and indeed some people would never forget it for you.

I am not talking about baseball but about such less glamorous activities as cutting turf or fishing or saving hay or corn. It wasn't too bad for the Texas Rangers – they could call on a substitute.

The bog is a rather different ball game. Four is the ideal number for cutting turf but you could manage with three – if one of those goes missing, it makes life very hard for the other two.

Nevertheless, I sympathise with Rick Leach and I half suspect that I understand his problem.

A few years ago a dear friend of mine walked off the stage in the middle of a very expensive production. The general verdict was that the drink was the cause.

On that night of his dramatic abdication my friend was as sober as I am this minute – and I am writing these words at five o'clock on a wet and windy morning.

That night in The Gaiety my friend was stricken with a disease familiar to most of us; it has no name but it is usually expressed in such words as: "What in the name of heaven am I doing here..."

Professional actors and professional sportsmen and professional writers are especially vulnerable to this arrow because they have a feeling of guilt about their trade. They cannot but believe that they are getting their money under false pretences. This would never happen to a turfcutter or a fisherman or a maker of puddings, either black or white.

And I can well understand why Mike Tyson goes walkabout now and then.

Friday, March 11, 1989

Stewards' enquiry at Knocknagoshel

Sometimes I am asked which sport I would pick if forced by a cruel master to confine myself to one – the answer is 'Racing'.

That game abounds in stories, not all of which – I need hardly mention – can be published.

On Tuesday last there was a little example of the sport's propensity for producing the bizarre.

Believe it or not, a non-runner named Sherwood Gunner romped home in the first race at Wetherby.

The explanation was alarmingly simple: The Press Association's man in Northern England had been misinformed.

He phoned the stable on Monday; the trainer agus a bhean were out; a lad in the yard answered.

Stable lads are an emphatic lot and though normally the P.A. man would have needed the word from a higher authority, he was satisfied that Sherwood Gunner was a non-runner.

And thus he was classified in Tuesday's morning papers.

People of a suspicious nature – and there are a lot of them about – will no doubt query the explanation.

And because Sherwood Gunner was backed down to 4/1, you may feel that this was yet another of racing's shady deeds.

I believe that the explanation is genuine, if only because there is no better way of drawing attention to a horse than have him appear in the field after being declared a non-runner.

And while all this was going on, the adulation that surrounds Desert Orchid continued to wax.

The worship has now reached a stage where one of the horse's co-owners, Richard Burridge, has decided to form a fan club.

The white horse – he is not really grey as officially described – is as popular here as in the other island, despite the tribal rivalry associated with the Cheltenham Festival.

Desert Orchid resides in one of Britain's loveliest regions, Hampshire.

If you wish to join, you should write to the Desert Orchid Fan Club, c/o David Elsworth, Whitsbury Manor Stables, near Fordingbridge, Hants, England.

Richard Burridge and his trainer David Elsworth are being bombarded with requests to retire their great horse.

Some people haven't a splink of sense; as Mr. Burridge said a few days ago in The Sporting Life "Retirement is possibly not the attraction for horses that it is for humans."

I doubt if it proves as pleasant for humans as most anticipate; you need to be very well equipped for retirement.

Desert Orchid is now ten; he has at least two more good seasons in him.

Obviously he relishes racing; it would be cruel to put him out on grass.

I think that I understand the motive of those who want him retired; they wish to see a dream enshrined.

And let us suppose that his form declines and that he runs in such little courses as Fontwell, you will hear people saying: "Oh dear, dear..."

And they will be wrong; it would be far worse to see him bored and listless in some winter field.

Some – perhaps many – horses love the excitement that goes with racing; if you doubt it, I will tell a little story I recited here before.

It concerns a horse that I cannot name because he had so many names – he showed his wares on the flapping circuit, in case you haven't guessed.

He was owned by my great friend, Tom Deane, a man whose

profession as a farmer didn't interfere unduly with his love of racing.

At the time of our story the horse in question was about fifteen. And for bad measure he had a lump about the size of a turnip on his near fore knee, occasioned by a collision with a pole.

You would think that he had seen enough of racing – far from it.

On the day of our story we were going to Knocknagoshel races, the centre-piece of The Harvest Festival.

Horse boxes were unknown in the flapper circuit in those days; Tom's noble steed travelled in a turf lorry, not inappropriate when you come to think of it.

As we came up the hill to the old village, the bunting hove into view – and the veteran's ears stood up and the eyes brightened and the nostrils flared.

He won his race that day too – but I must admit that there was some doubt about it.

An English woman whose horse had come second objected on the grounds that the veteran had gone inside one pole.

The stewards went into conclave; in simple language, they spent about a quarter of an hour over a few bottles of stout.

And then came the 'WINNER ALL RIGHT'.

What the innocent English lass didn't know was that all three stewards had backed Tom's horse.

That's another story – let us return to the adulation that surrounds some horses.

Arkle knew it: the amount and variety of the gifts sent to his stable were astonishing.

They included several of Nat Gould's novels, a bunch of heather guaranteed to have been picked in Lyrecrompane, and a signed photograph of The Queen Mother.

And there were several bottles of Lourdes water, numerous miraculous medals, bars of many kinds of chocolate, a photograph of Golden Miller (unsigned), and a quart of Newport poteen.

And for good measure the wonder horse got a rug made from peat moss, a hot-water bottle five gallons in volume, and an Elvis Presely single – 'Wooden Heart', in case you wish to know.

The arrival of Carvill's Hill and Maid Of Money – and of course Desert Orchid – has evoked endless discussions headlined "Which Was The Best Chaser Ever?"

Of course it can never be answered – that's among the reasons for its fascination.

On Monday I got involved: Arkle and Dawn Run seem to be the favourites – I am surprised that hardly anybody ever mentions Prince Regent or L'Escargot. For the time being we will let the horses sit.

One long-familiar face was missing from our Grand National – Paddy O'Brien is no longer in his earthly abode.

Paddy loved Fairyhouse, not least because of its homely and democratic flavour. And of course it was his local meeting – in his quiet way he was deeply proud of his origins.

He spent the first act of his working life in McDaid's, a pub that for some mysterious reason became the chapel of ease for writers and painters, real and alleged, and revolutionaries – all alleged.

Many of the most celebrated artists – in words and images – of the day were regulars there; they were treated like everybody else – firmly and courteously.

Reputations meant nothing to Paddy: in his countryman's scale of values a poet or a painter was no more important than a printer or a baker or a bus driver.

Nobody was privileged there, except some poor devil who was going through a bad time and needed minding.

When McDaid's changed hands, Paddy moved down to The Castle in South William Street, popularly know as Grogan's.

The regulars followed as devotedly as the children of Hamelin followed The Pied Piper but to a better end.

Thus McDaid's was reborn – only on a bigger scale.

You may not find Grogan's mentioned in the glossy tourist guides – but it is one of Dublin's greatest pubs.

You will find most of human life there – and the general atmosphere helps you to understand what Paris was like on the night after the fall of The Bastille.

There until a few months ago Paddy presided as quietly and as firmly as in McDaid's.

The other Paddy and Tommy must forgive me for thinking that he was the governor; it was only after his passing I found out that he was the second mate.

Paddy O'Brien was that kind of person; he was a born captain. We miss him.

Friday, October 6, 1989

Requiem for a friend

Air travel and television have wrought great changes in Irish life in this generation. When The Republic of Ireland travel to play Malta next month, hundreds will go with them and thousands will watch back at home.

If the teams had met on that little island thirty years ago, we would have had very few followers; the many at home would have to be content to "see" the game on the wireless.

When I first saw a soccer match in London, I had been travelling since seven o'clock on the previous morning.

Now it is only a journey of a few hours from Kerry to London - great surely is the change.

In this country there was always a fair degree of interest in cross-channel football; television and air travel hugely increased it.

And a new element came into our lives; football aficionados travel regularly to matches in Britain, especially to Liverpool and Manchester and London and Glasgow.

And the trip to watch their favourite team became a reward for boys - and indeed girls - who had done well in examinations.

It is all very civilised; you could say that it is a part of our culture.

And young people get to know places that to us were only names on the map when we were their age.

Frank McKenna was a pioneer of the football charter; Atlas Travel quickly became a greatly-respected agency.

The reason was simple: Frank gave a new dimension to the word 'professional' - and for good measure he had a marvellous personality.

I first met him on a grey Saturday in the Spring of 1974.

I had phoned Atlas on Friday afternoon and asked if there was a place on their charter for the following day. There was. And I would be given the flight ticket and the match ticket at the airport.

It seemed a rather vague arrangement - little did I know.

Anyhow, I turned up at the appointed time and was hardly ten seconds inside the check-in area when a youngish and neatly-built man with a great smile approached me.

He introduced himself; it was friendship at first sight.

Frank and myself were to travel to many parts of Britain and the continent in the intervening years.

Our last trip together was to Glasgow to watch Celtic play Rangers on that momentous day when Maurice Johnston made his debut for The Blues.

Frank might have been born to exemplify Stendhal's dictum: "The hallmark of high intelligence is the absence of fuss."

Nothing seemed any bother to him; what in other hands might be very complicated was made to appear simple by him.

Behind the relaxed, ever-pleasant exterior lay a genius for organisation.

And over the years the regular travellers on the Atlas trips became a kind of family.

They came from many walks of life but were united by their love of football.

Not all followed the same club - but it didn't matter; there was healthy rivalry - and the crack was always good.

Frank was a most dedicated supporter of Liverpool but I long suspected that Glasgow Celtic were his firstlings; that came with his Ulster heritage.

And he was never more at home than in Glasgow; he knew that old city as intimately as James Joyce knew Dublin. Sometimes we used to go over to Glasgow on morning flights and so have plenty of time before the match.

Then we would travel down into Ayrshire, into the lovely country that made Robbie Burns a poet.

And we used to have lunch and a few pints in a friendly little hotel near Troon; those days bring back very happy memories.

Of course there were the bad times too; the worst was that terrible night in the Heysel Stadium.

The match had to be put back for hours and all arrangements went overboard.

The trouble didn't end with the march; Brussels was a dangerous city that night, so much so that the Atlas charter had to take off from the cargo field.

Frank, aided by his great friend John Gahan of Aer Lingus, got us all back to Dublin.

The Hillsborough disaster, terrible though it was, didn't cause such complications; the big worry was about the worry of the people back at home.

And as soon as the match was abandoned, Frank and myself went to the nearest house and got on the phone to THE SUNDAY PRESS and RTE to let it be known that all the Atlas party were safe and well.

Frank was the proverbial man who does good deeds by stealth.

He was a tremendous friend to me; there were often times when I hadn't the money to go to a match - but it didn't matter; you could pay in your own good time.

And at producing match tickets, no matter how tight the circumstances, he was a magician.

There was an example on the day of Maurice Johnston's debut.

The interest – it is hardly the word – in that game bordered on the hysterical; it was, of course, all-ticket – and the word from Glasgow was that not a ticket was to be had by the Wednesday.

And yet a young man of my acquaintance took a chance; I met him on the Saturday morning on the flight from Dublin; he said – "You will get me a ticket."

Frank had gone over on an earlier flight but I had a fair idea of his whereabouts.

And of course he produced a ticket – and a good one.

Better was to follow; my young friend, hardly believing his luck, went off to meet three friends who were coming from Edinburgh - and found that they had no tickets. You can guess what followed.

They came to the hotel – and Frank, helped by Sean Ó Gallchoir of Aer Lingus, again worked the oracle.

I last met my great friend a few weeks ago as we came away from the All-Ireland football final; we had a few drinks and went our different ways.

It grieves me to think that I can never again ring 743092 and hear that friendly voice saying: "That will be all right, my old buddy."

He was like a father and a brother to me; he minded me, just as his brother and partner, Andy, minded me when I was in New York recently.

A great many people will miss him; one of our travelling family put it simply to me in Shanganagh cemetery last Tuesday: "A part of our life is over."

When last we met, Frank had just come back from Valetta where he had been looking at hotels in preparation for our match with Malta.

It was typical of him; he was a great professional and a great human being.

"Good night, sweet prince, and flights of angels sing thee to thy rest."

Saturday, May 20, 1989

Rural boys in Chicago

Yesterday I was talking about Chicago's pre-eminence in the realm of sport. Now read on...

This is the opening paragraph of a piece about The Windy City, written by Dirk Johnson in last Sunday's New York Times.

"In this city of Chicago sports fans do not do The Wave. They do not wave hankies. They do not paint themselves in team colours or wear gaudy costumes. They watch the game."

As William Shakespeare didn't say but might have said: "The game's the thing."

One of Chicago's two major newspapers, The Sun-Times, carries a wraparound sports section every Monday; the other news is confined to the inside pages; this is a fair indication of the city's culture.

And I like it. And another symptom is the extraordinary sales achieved by a book about sport, Rick Talley's "The Cubs of '69 – reflections of the team that should have been."

The Cubs, in case you haven't guessed, are one of the local baseball clubs; in that sad season of '69 they led the league by such a margin that they seemed uncatchable but in the last few weeks 'blew' a nine-game lead to The Mets.

The truth is that despite the great passion of the Chicagoans for sport, they have experienced little success in modern times.

The Chicago Bears won the Super Bowl in 1986 – that stands as a lonely landmark.

Now The Chicago Bulls are threatening to become the best team in basketball; "And" writes Dirk Johnson, "the noise that is shaking the rafters in Chicago Stadium is the thunder of hunger and gratitude."

They have never before got past the second round in the National Basketball Association play-offs; hence the extraordinary excitement they are now engendering.

And by far the biggest heroes now in the city by The Great Lakes are The Bears' coach, Mike Ditka, and The Bulls' scoring machine, Michael Jordan.

They may symbolise the city but they are hardly products of it: Ditka comes from the coal-mining belt of Pennsylvania; Jordan is a country boy from North Carolina.

Ditka and Jordan are said to have one thing in common; their backgrounds have given them a deep belief in the importance of sweat.

Jerry Drause, The Bulls' vice-president, says: "The Chicago fans are people who work hard and have high respect for the work ethic; they expect it in their players and they show them their appreciation for it."

I like that: I too know something about the work ethic – so much so that I have never in all my life gone on holiday.

Some kindly people tell me that all my life has been a holiday; they remind me of a Peruvian saying – "Nothing is any bother when somebody else has to do it."

In this context I remember especially the morning after I finished The Intermediate.

I came back down to earth over a thousand feet above sea level; I was guiding a mighty Clydesdale as we drew out the turf for a kinsman.

It was a momentous time – and I am thinking of more than the turf.

On my way home from Castlemartyr I had a few hours to spare in Cork and bought a copy of that great magazine, Picture Post.

It was devoted entirely to the Dunkirk evacuation – and a magnificent job it was; this was journalism at its best.

This was the time when Britain looked beaten; the unthinkable now seemed probable – the Germans would succeed where Napoleon had failed; they would cross the narrow sea.

And Winston Churchill, before Kevin Heffernan and Mick O'Dwyer and Sean Boylan, called for commitment.

"We will fight them on the beaches and in the woods and in the fields and in the streets and in the parks and in the laneways and in the cafés and in the pubs."

Legend tells us that when he finished that breathless paragraph, he turned to a colleague and whispered: "With what? Spades and shovels?"

It could have happened; Winston had an Irish sense of humour; not for nothing did he spend his early years in Dublin.

He more or less grew up in the Phoenix Park in the years when his old man was Lord Lieutenant.

The British aristocracy are marvellously indifferent to their offspring – and young Winston spent most of his time with the servant girls and others of the staff.

A great man he wasn't; he never got outside the mental parameters of his class – but a great humorist he certainly was.

And in New York recently I appreciated all the more one of his most famous one-liners.

Our Transatlantic neighbours can do strange things with words: for instance, the traffic lights have two instructions which can be a little confusing to newcomers.

They are 'WALK' and 'DON'T WALK' – and the second is especially misleading: if you took it literally, you would hail a cab.

Churchill greatly admired Franklin Roosevelt but there were times when communications threatened to break down.

As Winston said: "We are two kindred peoples divided by a common language."

Churchill is in my mind to-day because we are now approaching an anniversary of Dunkirk.

And this month in 1940 will always be remembered as 'Cloudless May'; that was among the reasons that the turf was dry so early.

And though there was an excellent chance of seeing the Nazi jackboot in the High Street in Knocknagoshel, we were more worried about the fate of Kerry's football team.

Cork weren't a mighty obstacle in those days; Kerry were almost guaranteed a place in the last four.

Kerry were reigning champions in that year of cloudless May and Dunkirk; they had just scrambled past Meath in the previous September.

They retained the title but not convincingly; they beat Galway by a point in a final which is chiefly remembered for the proliferation of fouls – 62 frees were awarded.

I have heard it labelled 'the first modern final' – you can make what you like out of that.

Now the slaughter of the innocents is upon us again – already for some counties the All-Ireland championships are over.

I sympathise with Carlow; they did an enormous amount of homework; at least in the short term it has proved in vain.

I know that I go on too much about this – but we must keep it up; silence might be interpreted as giving consent.

Tom Woulfe was a long time preaching against The Ban; his mission seemed hopeless – but eventually the wheel spun in his favour.

It is, of course, a national scandal that Tom isn't in high office in The G.A.A.

His amalgam of intelligence and imagination and integrity would have helped that grounded hulk to get back into clear water.

There were, however, always sufficient flat-earthers in high places to see that he didn't get into the corridors of power – he didn't even get to the entrance – they kept the door from the Woulfe.

Friday, September 8, 1989

Slow Boat To China

When I phoned Burgh Quay on Wednesday night and got the result from Windsor Park, I was not over pleased.

And a Hungary feeling came o'er me stealing, even though the mice were not squealing in my prison cell.

And I am now more convinced than ever that we will go to Malta needing full points.

And don't be so naive as to believe that those points are just there for the picking up.

The Maltese didn't impress when they were last here – but they were bent only on what our assessors call damage limitation.

On their own soil they will be an entirely different kettle of footballers.

And their crazy supporters – otherwise the nicest people in the world – will put an abundance of wind in their sails.

It is unlikely that Malta will ever win The World Cup or The Euro Cup; like Luxembourg and other small nations they play for prestige.

And when they meet us in a few weeks time, they will be under no more pressure than the goat at Puck Fair.

It is a ray of consolation that their new pitch is a model; our far more experienced players will have a stage to their liking.

Will we ever forget Taq 'Ali in the rare old times?

On the eve of that crazy game I was present at what was surely the most bizarre press conference of all time.

Peadar O'Driscoll, among others, had been to inspect the alleged pitch and returned with wondrous tales.

And out of a royal-blue duffel bag he produced a marvellous variety of objects he had picked up on his mission.

If you don't believe me, you can consult Charlie Stuart or Peter Byrne or Noel Dunne or some other layabout; they too were present.

Big Peadar's treasures included a china doll, an earthenware teapot, several abandoned kettles, a half of a tongs – I suppose you could call it a tong – and a bronze statue of the Emperor Napoleon the Third.

Malta is famous for its benign climate; on that evening, however, a dark wind blew up from Africa – and between the storm and the pitch it wasn't an occasion for one-touch football.

I do not wish to labour the issue but the man of the match was an old-fashioned inside-forward called Liam Brady.

A few minutes from the long whistle he made a most untypical lunge at his marker – and got the yellow card.

It was his second in the tournament and cost him his place in the game against Spain in Zaragossa.

We all do things in anger which we live to regret; I should know – it is the story of my life.

I have lost count of the number of times that I have left the Evening Press; I didn't say "I quit" – I just stormed out.

Once I even got as far a Bowe's pub before I repented – and it all reminds me of the famous story I have told here before about a neighbour called Dan.

Once upon a time his life was in considerable turmoil, mostly all of his own making – though you couldn't meet a more decent man.

And so he assembled his family and bade them all a sad farewell – he was going, he said, as far away from Kerry as he could.

And he would never come back – that's what the man said; now read on.

Dan didn't go to Australia; like many a good Kerryman before him, he got as far as Birmingham.

And like many a good Kerryman before and since he decided to sample the beer in New Street Station.

And when he put down his glass after the first quaff, the girl behind the bar said: "Tell me, Dan, how are they all in Knocknagoshel....?"

And there was another neighbour who made a similar odyssey: he must be nameless because the story concerns his wife.

They had a serious quarrel one night; I think it was about who should put out the cat – and in the best, or worst, Jack Charlton fashion he stormed out.

And he added a rider: "And I'll never come back." He was back in five minutes – and the good lady said: "What happened?" And he said: " 'Tis raining."

And of course you all know Gay Byrne's party piece. I've told it often before but so has he – and I have no doubt that he will tell it again.

It concerns two young lovers who were just married and, for good measure, who lived on the bank – the right, I think – of a navigable river.

One night they quarrelled as young – and old – lovers tend to do; he stormed out, long before it was popular or profitable.

Now it happened that he had a little boat; not for nothing did I put in that bit about the navigable river. And his parting shot was: "I'm going to row to China."

And he duly got into his little boat, took up the oars, and rowed furiously throughout the night; it was just as well that he forgot to undo the mooring.

He awoke in a lovely summer dawn; the chorus was in full chirp; God was in his heaven – all was right with the world.

And for good measure a sweet voice called out: "John Joe, darling, your breakfast is ready." And he said: "It's great – they know me in China."

Wednesday, October 6, 1993.

A Freeman now trapped at home

There was little or no organised football in the heyday of The Roman Empire but those who were employed to mint one-liners in those distant times might have foreseen the trauma of Brian Clough: "Whom the gods wish to destroy, they first make mad."

If we are to believe most of what we read and hear, this modern version of Robin Hood is now a lost soul without even a Little John or an Alan-a-Dale to stand by him.

He seems the victim of a cruel paradox; he is a freeman of a lovely city but is trapped in his home, inhibited from venturing out lest he suffer the slings and arrows of outrageous criticism.

A few years ago while undergoing interrogation by a certain Joe Duffy,

I was asked to name my favourite football manager. I didn't hesitate – "Brian Clough."

Matt Busby and Bill Shankly and Bob Paisley achieved an abundance of success with clubs that were "natural" members of The Round Table; Clough achieved his with clubs and seemed destined to be onlookers at football's feast.

And he did so by producing adventurous football; Clough grew up in a woefully-deprived part of Britain but emerged from it as a poet; it was as if a rose tree sprouted out of a slag heap.

Those of us who are older remember him as a brilliant golador, an old-fashioned centre-forward with a gift for snapping up unconsidered chances and turning them into goals.

He seemed all set for football's higher plateaus – The First Division, as it was then, and the international arena.

Then came the proverbial shears of fate; injury grounded the soaring eagle – he would never fly again.

His second career brought him fame and glory and the kind of money that he could hardly have made as a player – and yet I cannot help suspecting that it didn't bring him satisfaction.

No matter how much success a teacher achieves, he remains prey to a niggling doubt; he cannot help feeling that his disciples might have done just as well with someone else.

And of course no matter how much Clough resorted to positive thinking, he couldn't but ponder on what might have been, on the pitch as distinct from the bench.

Clough's players, especially in the later years, sometimes didn't see him between one match and the next; this suggests that he didn't enjoy teaching; yes, I know, there is a more popular explanation.

And perhaps the latter explanation is nearer the mark.

We have been hearing for years that Clough has a drink problem; seemingly rumour is now accepted as fact.

I suppose we shouldn't be surprised; Tommy Docherty's words come to mind – "In this business you either drink or go mad. And I have no intention of going mad."

Brian Clough is intelligent but he is hardly an intellectual; I doubt if he takes much pleasure in reading or in contemplation.

He lives in a part of the country where there is great angling water but I doubt if he is a follower of Izaak Walton.

And when a man has a surplus of money and time, you shouldn't be too hard on him if he seeks refuge in fantasies.

You could, I suppose, argue that Clough's quiver of trophies should be a great solace in middle age – seemingly it isn't.

He lost his last war; two years ago he threatened to retire – he went the proverbial ford too far.

Forest were ravaged by injuries last season; even Clough's genius – or what remained of it – couldn't arrest the spiral. It was a bad way to go out.

In the end he couldn't articulate his little spiels for the local electricity board and Shredded Wheat. The tabloids have had a beano.

Now you might say, if you were in the mood for cliches, it's time for all his friends to rally around – and so it is, only that he seems to have no friends.

Believe it or not, he never had a drink with Peter Taylor, the man who for so many years was his Sancho Panza; seemingly their wives never even met.

Perhaps it isn't true to say that Clough has no friends: many of my colleagues claim to be close to him – but that to me is a dubious kind of friendship; it is rather like that between Albert Reynolds and Dick Spring.

A dear friend of mine, a brilliant player who was a member of England's squad for the finals of the 1966 World Cup, will tell you that Brian Clough is eminently equipped to write the inverse of Dale Carnegie's handbook – How To Make Enemies And Not Influence People.

He played under the great man and didn't especially enjoy the experience.

Brian Clough is still a comparatively young man; he seems "magnificently unprepared for the long littleness of life."

Last Monday week's World In Action hardly made enjoyable viewing for this modern Robin Hood.

It suggested that he robbed the poor to feed the rich – the rich, in this case, being himself.

The charge was not new: we remember the accusation of embezzlement when he was with Derby County. And of course there was the case of Paddy Mulligan's benefit and the brown paper bag.

And there is the story told by Graham Alston, a director of Scunthorpe in the eighties; he alleges that Clough demanded £1,500 to take Forest to Scunthorpe for a friendly in 1982.

The receipts came to a meagre £10,000. Clough, accompanied by Forest's chairman, Maurice Roworth, took his money and said "Thank you very much."

And yet I prefer to remember Brian Clough as a great judge who bought shrewdly and practised a brilliant philosophy of football.

I will allow the last words to Geoff Boycott: "If Brian Clough walked into the dressing room before a game, I would score a century every time."

Wednesday, September 19, 1993.

Black humour – Bruno style

Cardiff is a small friendly city that has seen better times: coal and steel are only memories; in the great days The River Taff carried so much coaldust and steeldust that even the eels threatened to forsake it; now it is pure and lucid; nevertheless, Cardiff will for a few hours this weekend become for some people the capital of the world.

Those people are, of course, the aficionados of pugilism – the Fancy, as our old friend William Hazlitt labelled them.

In The Arms Park or, if you like, The National Stadium, two Britons will make history; never before have two natives of our neighbouring isle fought for the heavyweight title of the world.

Both are brown of skin and were born in London of Jamaican parents; each lost his father at an early age; both came to boxing by a familiar route – it offered an escape from the semi-criminal life of the streets.

There, apart from their great physical presence, the resemblance ends – or at least seems to end.

Lennox Lewis is educated and intelligent; Frank Bruno is deemed a big baby – except of course when he climbs into the ring.

We are regularly assured that he is bumbling, if not inarticulate; those people infected with the disease known as racism love him – he corresponds to their image of the backward brown boy.

Those who know him well will tell you that Big Frank is about as innocent as an accountant or a publican or a pig buyer or a Cavan farmer or a bookie, not to mention a bookie's clerk.

With those great big eyes and the wide mouth and the seeming shyness, he comes over on television as a large-size Uncle Tom; while all this is going on, he is laughing all the way to the stock exchange.

Bruno is what is known as a family man; Lewis is unmarried; his name has never been associated with some model or star, nor indeed with any girl friend or friend girl.

He lives with his mother, a devout member of the Pentecostal church; her name is Violet but she is a very strong person.

She saw to it that he got a fair education; it is just as important that she is a brilliant cook, even by West Indian standards.

Even when he was preparing for bouts in the USA and training there, she cooked his every bit; now she is in Cardiff to save her son fr om the terrors of Welsh cuisine.

The popular image of pugilists, especially heavyweights, is unflattering: they are seen as gifted with muscle at the expense of mind; this perception is to some degree rooted in begrudgery; people envy pugilists their skill and bravery – as a compensation they label them dim-witted.

There is no dearth of examples to query this image: Jack Johnson was alarmingly intelligent; Muhammad Ali was mesmerisingly articulate; Gene Tunney was an intellectual to the point of embarrassing people.

Lennox Lewis, unlike Tunney, is not threatening to go around the world lecturing on Shakespeare; he is so confident of his intellectual powers that he feels no need to put out flags.

He plays chess; an even greater symbol of his intelligence is that he plays draughts, the great boardgame of rural Ireland before the advent of television.

Nevertheless, this 28-year-old son of London's East End can fight a bit too; he won the Olympic heavyweight title in Seoul and is current champion of the world.

Watchers of Sky, as distinct from astronomers and astrologers, are well aware of his prowess; as far back as three years ago he was obviously championship material.

Of course he was fed on the usual diet of has-beens and never-would-bes but this couldn't disguise his gifts; he has a marvellous physique and the kind of hand speed and foot speed rare in such big men.

His time of trial came when he went into the roped rectangle, oddly called the ring, with Donovan Ruddock.

Ruddock had been in with the greats; you couldn't have found a more genuine examiner for an upcomer; Lewis blew him away in a few minutes.

He isn't undisputed world champion; he holds The World Boxing Council's version – he got it by default when Riddick Bowe refused to take part in a mandatory defence of his title.

Nevertheless, he is generally recognised as the number one: he defeated Bowe in the Seoul final – and the American's refusal to meet him is seen as complimentary.

Lewis is a counter puncher; those who saw the fight with Ruddock need no telling; the American opened with a flurry of big punches – Lewis felled him with a single blow.

His trainer, Pepe Correa, has the utmost confidence in Lewis; he should know – he worked with an immortal, Sugar Ray Leonard.

He says of his pupil: "His greatest talent is his ability to stay cool, almost relaxed, in the ring."

Where does all this leave Bruno? Nobody has ever accused Big Frank of being a boxer but he hasn't done too badly.

The experts will tell you that he could have been world champion; he hooked a great fish called Mike Tyson but lost him on the lip of the landing net.

The video seems to bear the experts out: Tyson was rocking but Bruno didn't realise it and failed to follow up; that night in Las Vegas four years ago was probably the apex of his career.

His record is impressive, if in a rather negative way; he has lost to such fearsome opponents as Bonecrusher Smith and Tim Witherspoon and, of course, Tyson – he lost impressively.

He is very brave and very strong and at 32 is probably at his physical peak.

Lewis is 6' 5" and wights $16^{1}/_{2}$ stone; Bruno is 6' 3" and about the same weight.

The general opinion is that this fight in the very early hours of Sunday morning will last only a few rounds.

The scenario may be confounded; Lewis could be content to "box clever" as he did last May when he outpointed Tony Tucker.

If he wins, it's almost certain that he will meet Riddick Bowe, holder of the IBF and WBA titles, in a "unifying" bout. There is also a certain Tommy Morrison – he is WBO champion.

Things were simpler in those days when we got out of bed to listen to fights on the wireless.

Friday, October 8, 1993

Lewis still has some way to go

Will Britain ever have a heavyweight champion of the world? The question evokes a famous story about Joe Beckett.

Joe, in case you didn't know, was an English prizefighter in the first quarter of this century.

One night when he was in the ring for a fight on the Continent, the M.C. said quietly that he would announce him as "Undisputed champion of Great Britain."

"No" said Joe "Just announce me as 'British champion'." He had a point.

The much-hyped fight in the early hours of last Sunday morning was dangerously close to being an anti-climax.

The crowd was less than expected ;this was hardly surprising – an open-air fight on a cold wet night in Cardiff isn't irresistibly attractive.

There was another cause for all those unsold tickets; few took Frank Bruno seriously – he was seen less as a contender than a decent man in quest of a bonanza for his retirement.

And there was another factor; Lennox Lewis is not seen as a true Briton, not on account of his Jamaican parentage but because he has got so much of his pugilistic education on the other side of The Atlantic.

And where does all this leave Bob Fitzsimons? He was undisputed heavyweight champion of the world.

He too wasn't seen as a true Briton; his parents had emigrated from Wexford to Cornwall – and he spent most of his life in Australia and America.

If Lennox Lewis gets past Tommy Morrison and Riddick Bowe, he will be undisputed champion and may then be generally accepted back at home as a true Briton.

A contributory factor to the sense of near anti-climax last weekend was the display of Lewis.

He didn't look likely to conquer America's best and destroy the Transatlantic myth which sees British heavyweights as congenitally inferior.

When Tommy Farr took Joe Louis over fifteen hard rounds, he shook this myth but that was a long time ago. The myth got an abundance of support in the meantime.

Don Cockell put up a brave show against Rocky Marciano – but wasn't a contender.

Frank Bruno had a momentary chance of becoming world champion when he met Mike Tyson but it is doubtful if he would have lasted long on the throne.

We will pass over Joe Bugner and the others who were no more than pretenders.

It is almost certain that Bruno will never again appear in the centre court.

Those heavyweights who campaign long after their great days are part of American culture.

If Big Frank has bowed out, he did so with grace and dignity – and with humour. "Nothing in his life became him like the leaving."

And he confounded those, many of them greatly-respected experts, who have long been rather dismissive of his pugilistic ability.

He shed his image as a powerful brawler; he set out with a plan and stuck to it – he boxed so well that he was probably level on points at the start of that fatal seventh round.

Last Wednesday I diverged from the general scenario and wrote that I expected Lewis to play safe and bide his time.

My reason was obvious; when you have such an advantage in reach as Lewis had, you are safer at some distance from Bruno – Big Frank is not environment friendly.

And of course there was the question of Bruno's stamina – or lack of it.

Last weekend's fight was almost a copy of Bruno's clash with Tim Witherspoon; once again he did well until he ran short of steam.

I know a few acquaintances who have a theory about Frank's lack of stamina; I hasten to add that these same acquaintances have theories about almost everything.

Their theory is this: Bruno's legs are not strong enough to support his great body for more than seven or eight rounds or so.

They will tell you that he is weak from the knees down – I don't know. My acquaintances are experts in this field.

And those same experts on the human physique will tell you that this is quite common in brown-skinned and black-skinned people.

It is an interesting theory. Where does it leave Muhammad Ali and Mike Tyson? They are noticeably free from this alleged flaw.

My expert acquaintances have an explanation: Ali and Tyson have European blood – again, I don't know.

I managed to watch the fight – in a pub, the name of which wild horses, even at long prices, will not drag from me.

Our licensing law is an ass; I take that back – it isn't fair to poor oul' Neddy. I know enough about the donkey to be aware that he is not an ass.

I am fairly confident that our licensing laws will soon be no more than a memory of our dark past.

Those people in Brussels who are more and more affecting our lives will almost certainly introduce the hours of opening and closing that prevail on the continent.

I will refer to another aspect of the Brussels bureaucracy; I foresee a day when pugilism will be banned.

Many cottage industries, in the true sense of the label, have incurred their thumbs down.

Pugilism, I fear, will go the way of all flesh. Then, of course, it will go underground.

Tuesday, October 12, 1993.

How to wren-ch the eagle's glory

You shouldn't believe all you hear – especially in the rainy season; I wasn't in Brussels on the eve of Waterloo, nor was I in Dublin on the run-up to The Battle Of Clontarf.

Nevertheless, I have a fair idea of the atmosphere that prevailed on those occasions: I was in Kerry on the second Sunday in September 1982.

Our county team in Gaelic football had won four successive All-Irelands; they were on the brink of an historic five-in-a-row.

It would be impossible to exaggerate in expressing the sense of triumphalism; my neighbours, men and women and cats and dogs, were smacking their lips in anticipation of a seventy-minute lap of honour.

'Five in a row' dominated every aspect of life in The Kingdom.

Ballads were being composed and recorded. Cakes with the relevant motif were being baked. Black puddings – and even white puddings – were on display in strings of five.

All kinds of garments were being emblazoned with that magic number – tee shirts, coffee shirts, cocoa shirts, boxer's shorts, wrestler's shorts, long johns, all kinds of underwear and overwear.

As I happened to be in Killarney, I went up to the park to see the final rehearsal.

It took the form of a game between the dream team and the understudies. The chosen fifteen won by 5-14 to 0-7. God was in his heaven – all was right with the world.

I have a vivid memory of Paudie O'Shea waving to me as he came off the pitch; he was walking on land because no water was available.

I adjourned to Jimmy O'Brien's to diminish my mesmerisation.

And in that alarmingly hospitable tavern I found myself in the midst of an orgy of aficionados.

In a moment of wild indiscretion I ventured to say that Offaly were quietly confident.

An awesome silence ensued; an infidel had been unveiled in Mecca.

When the shock had subsided, a veteran of many summers and almost as many winters said: "We will not hear of defeat."

I maintained a stoic silence but said to myself: "You may not hear of defeat – but you could read about it."

And so it came to pass: Kerry were four points ahead with six minutes to go; now read on.

Matt The Thresher kept his marvellous head and took points from two frees when a lesser man would have sought a goal.

Two minutes remained. A long ball dropped about fifteen yards from Kerry's goal – suddenly a fearsome intuition smote me.

And I said to a friend girl – as distinct from a girl friend – "We're done for."

I know that you are not supposed to end a sentence with a preposition – but it was a moment of terrible stress.

A Kerry defender, whom I prefer not to name, rose for the ball; so did Seamus Darby who had been sent on only five minutes previously.

Suddenly wee Seamus was in possession; his right foot spoke.

The ball sped away about shoulder high to Charlie Neligan's left; my friend and neighbour could only make a despairing leap.

And as I tottered away from Croke Park, a chapter from an old school reader came into my mind.

Do you remember readers . . . They were books, not people.

They were the days of parsing and analysis, of grammar and punctuations, the days when we learned poetry "off by heart" and when the apostrophe was alive and well.

This chapter, or lesson, if you like, told about a certain World Cup; it happened before that label was minted. Some exceptionally enterprising promoter, the Don King of his day, organised it.

It was to decide which bird could fly the highest.

There was an enormous entry; they came from all quarters and eighths of the globe.

And precisely at eight o'clock on the morning of Midsummer Day the tapes went up.

So did the birds; the sky darkened; there was a magnificent symphony of wings. All through that long day when all the world was young, the contest waged.

Some birds weren't, of course, contenders atall; they just entered for the crack.

When people were bringing in the cows for milking, only five birds were in contention.

You have probably guessed who they were – a peregrine falcon, a sparrow hawk, a swallow, a swift, and an eagle.

The cows were back in their pastures: children were being put to bed (all this was before television) and rooks were making their way to the leafy wood – the contest went on and on.

It was almost dusk when at last the peregrine falcon and the sparrow hawk and the swallow and the swift conceded in the best tradition of candidates for The White House.

And the eagle with a triumphant flourish of his wings said: "I am the king".

Little did he know: suddenly a voice from about a foot above him said: "No way – I am the king".

A wren had stowed away in the eagle's plumage; he was the Seamus Darby of his day.

There was no objection; there wasn't even a stewards' enquiry.

And that is why we hear a chant every St. Stephen's Day which begins: "The wren, the wren, the king of all birds".

Friday, February 23, 1990

Joe, Gentle Giant from Tiger Bay

The Scots and their cousins across The North Channel have, at least in the realm of sport, the reputation of being self-destructive; examples spring readily to mind.

Benny Lynch was a brilliant flyweight – and was also the proverbial comet that shot across the sky and vanished without trace.

Jackie Paterson was world champion in that same division; he lost the title to Rinty Monahan – and not long after he lost his life in a pub brawl.

Rinty, a decent little man whom I often met in his show business days, at least died in bed – but he too had a remarkable talent for not being able to hold onto money.

I need hardly mention George Best, the Dylan Thomas of football; Best too is a decent man who has found it impossible to come to terms with his genius.

Our nearest neighbours across The Irish Sea have the name of being well able to mind their money; indeed if you were to believe Evelyn Waugh, you would see them not only as miserly but cute and even sly.

I have my doubts: indeed I have long suspected that the Welsh share a certain streak of madness with ourselves: they too have sporting heroes who seemed to find their later lives a saddening anti-climax.

John Charles was one of the best all-round soccer players of all time; his career might have been scripted by the obscure genius who created Roy of the Rovers – he didn't settle too well into life off the pitch.

John, however, fulfilled himself in his profession; his neighbour Joe Erskine who departed this world a few days ago did not.

By ordinary standards Joe had a fine career but he wasn't ordinary: in what is often described as the golden era of heavyweight boxing in Britain he was the most talented – but not the most successful.

Joe hadn't what is known as a drink problem but he was very fond of beer and much preferred the public house to the gymnasium.

Indeed if Joe had trained diligently, he might have been more than a good heavyweight – he could have been world champion in the lightheavy division.

A feature of that "golden era" of British heavyweights was that some of the protagonists were not really heavyweights atall.

Joe Erskine could have fought at lightheavy; so too could Johnny Williams; so could Henry Cooper.

That truth dawned on me forcibly one night long ago when I found myself next to him in the press bar at Wembley.

Indeed if ever there was a 'natural lightheavy', it was our 'Enry.

I saw our reflections in the mirror and could hardly believe that the man next to me had been in the ring with Muhammad Ali – or Cassius Clay as he was then.

Let us return to Joe Erskine. He was born in Tiger Bay, a part of Cardiff that has been outrageously romanticised. Invariably it is described as 'a tough district'; in fact, it is an ordinary working-class environ.

It has long had a considerable "coloured" element; Shirley Bassey is a daughter of the quarter – but Tiger Bay is no more tough than Ringsend or Portobello or Inchicore.

My knowledge of Joe as a pugilist is confined to film; he was a supreme examplar of what is known as the British style.

In short, he brought flesh to an old definition – 'The noble art of self-defence...'

He was a beautiful mover and thus very difficult to hit.

He lacked what our American friends call a Sunday punch; he won most of his fights on points.

He took the British championship from Johnny Williams in 1956. Johnny was reputed to be a gypsy; he wasn't but he was to some extent an intinerant – he had fought in the booths.

He was born in a little town called Barmouth; it is just across the sea from Arklow; on some nights you can see its lights from the Wicklow mountains.

Johnny was legendary for his toughness – but that night long ago he found Joe's speed of hand and foot too much.

The heavyweight scene in Britain now resembles Old Mother Hubbard's Cupboard; it was well stocked in Joe's time. Three of its occupants were Welsh – Joe and Johnny and Dick Richardson.

And then there was Henry Cooper and Brian London and such good journeymen as Alex Buxton and Billy Walker and Nosher Powell.

Joe Erskine battled with Henry Cooper five times; he lost the rubber 3-2. The last bout was his saddest; he retired at the end of the fifth round.

I know from my Cardiff friends that Joe was a very nice man – a gentle giant, only that he wasn't a giant atall.

On Tuesday last *The Independent* paid him a remarkable tribute; it carried two obituaries – one in the sports section and one in the features department.

It was typical of that fine young paper; it admires class because it exudes that same quality itself.

Joe Erskine lived almost all of his life in his beloved Cardiff; he died there all alone in a modest flat; he was 56.

And why, you may ask, didn't Joe and others of his era campaign as lightheavies; the answer is simple – the heavyweight division has always been the most glamorous and hence, of course, the most lucrative.

———

Tuesday, May 15, 1990

Liam made the most of his gifts

Small boys and even big boys look on the life of a professional footballer as the ideal existence – little do they know.

It is at best an unnatural life – and at worst a kind of living purgatory.

And if you believe that Liam Brady has dwelt for about 20 years in The Promised Land, you must think again.

Of course by any standards he has had a fabulous career – but the gods have a wry sense of humour and tend to exact a price for their seeming gifts.

Cast your mind back a few years and remember our scenario for the Euro and World Cups.

We had it all mapped out – our team would be built around David O'Leary, Mark Lawrenson, Frank Stapleton, and Liam Brady.

And when at last we crossed The Red Sea, only Frank, the eternal survivor, was on board.

Injury had guillotined Mark's career; Liam was in the repair shop; David was the victim of selectorial myopia.

And young lads who were hardly a wet season in football partook of the glory in West Germany.

Such is life; irony is always lurking around the corner.

It wasn't Liam's first encounter with that prankster.

In his late career at Highbury he knew a season that promised a rich harvest – and yielded nothing.

Arsenal were chasing a great treble – FA Cup and League and European Cup-Winners' Cup.

They ended up all too aware of what Tantalus* had suffered.

Of course Liam Brady has huge entries on the credit side of the book.

He is one of the few who has gone into folklore by having an English Cup Final labelled with his name.

Everybody remembers the 1979 decider as Liam Brady's Final.

And almost everybody deems his display on the momentous day as his greatest ever..

I do not much relish the role of non-conformist – but for once I cannot concur.

And I think of a grey windy afternoon at Highbury long ago when Arsenal were playing Everton in The League.

It was a splendid game – and ended 2-2.

Liam dominated those 90 minutes as much as an individual can – and for great measure scored an astonishing goal.

It came in the last quarter and was scored at The North End, just below Arsenal's devoted Bank.

Liam brought the ball down the inside-right corridor; all the defenders were present and correct – danger seemed remote.

Suddenly, about 25 yards from goal, Liam let fly with his right foot – the ball roared high into the net.

I can still see the astonishment on his immediate marker's face. Was it Colin Todd?

Until that moment everybody in football and a great many outside it looked on Liam's right foot as illiterate.

I remember the heading on my piece on the following Monday – 'LIAM, KING OF HIGHBURY'.

They were great days for the Irish in London or thereabouts.

I remember a Saturday when Arsenal fielded seven players from this small island.

Of course you can name them – Pat Jennings, Pat Rice, John Devine, Sammy Nelson, David O'Leary, Liam Brady, and Frank Stapleton.

I must say in passing that it seemed unreal last Saturday to watch Manchester Untied playing without an Irishman on board.

That's another story; it seems strange now to see The Republic playing without Liam.

Every footballer dreams of ending his career on the highest possible note – it doesn't always work out that way.

Liam's international career ended in just about the saddest possible way.

That day at Lansdowne Road I recalled a fragment from William Shakespeare – "The deep damnation of his taking off."

It was a bad way to go; I have no wish to re-open old wounds – but our Jack boobed in publicly humiliating a great player.

And his excuse was pathetic; if he had allowed Liam to remain on until the interval, the West Germans might have scored again.

It was, after all, only a friendly; Jack shouldn't have been so worried about keeping his long unbeaten run intact.

And even though I know that Liam needn't worry about the threatened rise in the price of black pudding, I welcome his testimonial.

It provides him with a worthy stage on which to make his farewell bow.

And I would give more than an old penny for Liam's thoughts as he walks off the pitch tomorrow evening.

He has come a very long way since the day his parents escorted him out to Collinstown and put him on the plane for Heathrow.

He was fifteen: it is still a young age; 20 years ago at fifteen you were little more than a child.

I was a few years older when first I encountered London – and I can still remember the fear that smote me as the train from Fishguard neared the gates of the great capital.

I soon lost my dread of London and came to love the place – but I didn't start out there as an apprentice professional footballer.

Of course Liam had wonderful talent. And of course he knew it – but talent didn't guarantee that he would survive in that fiercely competitive world.

I have known marvellously-gifted players who didn't; I have a neighbour who had such an amalgam of physique and skill that he could have made a good living across The Irish Sea – he lasted only a few weeks.

You need great will power and infinite patience – and above all you need the mental equipment to fight off man's most insidious enemy, loneliness.

Liam survived – and did a great deal more: he is that rare Irishman – he made the most of his gifts.

We tend to suspect fulfilment; we incline towards those who have within them the Hamlet-like proclivity towards self-destruction.

Liam has always possessed great discipline – he has walked down mean fields without being mean himself.

Some people will tell you that he was – or is – our greatest-ever footballer. That kind of hype is strictly for the birds – if only because no one amongst us has seen them all.

All I will say is that he was a great player and a marvellously entertaining player.

In an age when subtlety is suspect he cherished the old-fashioned approach; he might have laid the foundation of his craft on a Brazilian beach rather than in the playing fields of Dublin.

That winkle-picking left foot gave us myriad moments of delight – and caused many an opponent to wonder if the laws of physics had been changed overnight.

* The Greek God who was condemned to suffer the ultimate in frustration: for example, whenever he reached for grapes, they moved away from him.

Friday, 25 October, 1991

A wonderful Constitution . . .

Whenever rugby characters are mentioned, a certain Charlie Teehan is usually at the head of the poll; he was one of the few people who could justly be deemed a legend in his own lifetime.

Charlie's origins were in the hill country between Castle Island and Killarney; he was a distant cousin of mine; I can hear you saying: "Sure aren't ye all cousins in Kerry . . ."

He went to school in Cork and made his name with Presentation College; he was a brilliant hooker in an era when hooking was a very subtle art.

From Presentation he went to Cork University; he posed there as a medical student; in fact, he was studying rugby.

In his first year in college he was capped for Ireland; he played against

England and Scotland and Wales – France were then outlawed for violent play.

The year was 1939; by September, Hitler was heading for Danzig – and Paddy for Holyhead; Charlie Teehan abandoned his medical studies and enlisted in The British Army.

He ended his career as a soldier in the African desert.

He came back to Cork; like many a soldier he found life difficult in the civilian world; soldiering doesn't qualify you for anything.

He worked at a variety of jobs and resumed his rugby career with Cork Constitution.

Charlie didn't mind himself; he fell into bad health and had to go to a sanatorium.

There his luck took a great turn; he married his doctor; she got him to go back to the university.

He abandoned his careless ways and lost no time in qualifying as a dentist. For good measure he coached U.C.C. to win two Munster Cups.

I lost all track of Charlie until one Saturday morning a few years ago.

I was in Fleet Street (of fond and loving memory) in The Irish Press office; the phone rang; I was amazed to hear from Charlie.

He was ringing from Preston; he had a good job with Lanchashire County Council.

He asked me to help him write the story of his life; of course I agreed – alas, a few months later Charlie Teehan departed this mortal world.

You can read about him and many other fine players in a history of Cork Constitution, written by Edmund Van Esbeck and published a few weeks ago.

In a photograph of the Constitution team that won the Munster Cup in 1946 you will see Charlie standing next to Derry Crowley – it was no coincidence.

"Starry" simply was another tremendous character; he was also a great player; how he managed to avoid being picked for Ireland is a major mystery.

It is a consolation that he is immortalised in that rather ribald ballad, "The Boys of Fair Hill".

J. C. Daly was another member of that great generation; he immortalised himself by scoring the try that won The Triple Crown at Ravenhill in 1948.

Jack was a native of Cobh and like many a son of that hill-blessed town he served in The British Navy.

When the war was over, he returned home and joined Constitution.

There is a story about him which I am assured is true.

Batt Hayes was an outstanding prop on that team. And therein hangs the tale.

Constitution were due to play in Dublin in late 1946; some of the national selectors decided to cast an eye on Batt; he played well but it was the other prop who more impressed.

And thus Jack Daly sprang to fame. Like Charlie Teehan he found it hard to make a living in the civilian world; he turned professional in 1948.

Constitution have carved many famous victories in the Munster Cup; none was more celebrated than that in the final of 1961 – because it was so unexpected.

Constitution were in a trough at the time; Garryowen, their opponents in the final, were on a crest – and the game was in Thomond Park.

Garryowen had an especially strong loose trio – Noel Murphy and Tim McGrath and my Castle Island team-mate, Sean Brosnan.

Noel was then working in Limerick and found himself playing against his old club.

The Constitution pack rose above themselves and managed to tie down that formidable loose trio.

And as play went deep into the last quarter, the Cork side were leading 9-5 – but under fierce pressure.

Constitution made a break-out and got a penalty on the half-way; Ray Hennessy, their captain, planted it. That huge kick decided the game.

Saturday, December 23, 1989

Much to the disappointment of doctors and bonesetters

Sometime someone will write the history of Gaelic football – and tell it as it was; it will not be an altogether pretty story.

Eoghan Corry might be the man; his new book, 'Catch and Kick', suggests that he is willing to paint warts and all.

Of course it cannot be regarded as a history of our favourite game; it is more of a sighting shot.

In its 340 pages my colleague covers a vast amount of territory – inevitably it has to skim the surface at times.

Eoghan has such an easy and unpretentious style that you would never guess that he is a journalist.

And in the sub-language of the publishing business his book is a great read.

The early chapters fascinated me most; the origin and evolution of Gaelic football is a great theme.

The early form of the game was, believe it or not, rugby pure and simple – if anything is ever pure.

There is not a doubt in the world about this.

P.D. Mehigan, otherwise Carbery, quotes newspaper accounts of early games; they could have been played in Twickenham or The Arms Park.

I am often asked why Kerry have been so successful at Gaelic football – I doubt if there is a simple explanation.

Perhaps they had a flying start: Rugby was very strong in several parts of the county before Michael Cusack got his brainwave.

And it was perhaps easier for my countymen to adapt when the game evolved or otherwise into the form familiar this century.

Why Rugby was so strong in Kerry about a hundred years ago I do not know.

Perhaps it may have something to do with the Holy Ghost Fathers; Rockwell College usually had a fair complement of Kerry lads.

Certainly it had little to do with the British presence: my own native place has a great rugby tradition – but it was never a garrison town.

And, of course, Kerry was a heartland of Caid, the ancient game of which Rugby is a distilled version.

Eoghan Corry, needless to mention, did his homework on Caid.

And of course he mentions the remarkable priest, Father Liam Ferris, a man whom I was privileged to know.

He was famous for many reasons, including a history of the world in which The French Revolution got a whole footnote all to itself.

He also wrote a history of Caid, a game which he loved with excessive passion.

He tried to revive it and indeed organised a few games.

Eoghan tells us that the good priest's attempts at revival were very successful in the Christmas of 1926-'27.

I suppose it all depends on what you mean by 'successful'.

It is true that the matches aroused enormous interest, especially when played, if that is the word, by teams, if that is the word, from either side of the Cork-Kerry border.

The revival wasn't continued, much to the regret of the local doctors and bone-setters.

Caid was not so much a game as a kind of warfare.

And yet Father Liam accused Michael Cusack of committing an act of treachery when he invented Gaelic football.

In an oft-quoted judgement he said that Cusack had abolished the ancient game with one stroke of a pen.

Gaelic football grew like a beanstalk in a moist May, probably because it was so easy to understand and to play with satisfaction.

It is, of course, a game which owes a great deal to Rugby and Soccer; only the most obdurate of chauvinists can deny that.

And it is about as traditional as the sewing machine and the gramophone and the safety pin, not to mention the typewriter and the telephone and the stickless frying-pan.

Life is never short of irony: The Ban excluded rugby players from the G.A.A. even though it was the modern form of an ancient Irish game.

Some of our traditionalists will not thank Eoghan Corry for spilling the green beans.

Nor will the guardians of the national shrine be pleased that he doesn't gloss over some rather unsavoury episodes in the history of the 'ancient' game.

Of course not everybody down the years was blinded by sham patriotism.

Eamon de Valera, for example, provoked the wrath of the ancient Gaelic gods when he suggested that Rugby was the game most suited to Irish people.

Sean McEntee was equally bold: "I would like every Irishman to play the game that most appeals to him and I have no sympathy with the policy of exclusion pursued by The Gaelic Athletic Association."

They were brave words from a politician in the dark year of 1931.

My colleague Eoghan is not without a sense of humour; heaven knows, as a follower of Kildare's football fortunes he needs it.

And he has dedicated his book to the next team from his native county to win an All-Ireland.

'Catch and Kick' isn't without errors; these will no doubt be corrected when it goes into the next editions, as it surely will.

Nor is it without some darkly amusing tales.

You will read about Kerry's expedition to the U.S.A. in 1927.

It was hardly a success – and one aspect of it shocked some people back at home, at least in the South-West.

That Kerry team had a fabulous record; their team-sheet reads like a litany of folk-heroes – they were deemed unbeatable.

Unbeatable? They lost the first game to New York by 3-11 to 1-7 – and the second by 12 points to three.

Worse was to follow: the promoter, a former baseball manager called Ted Sullivan, disappeared into thick air – so did all the receipts of the tour.

A benefit game was arranged; New York won again, this time by 2-5 to 2-1. 'A donation from the Kerry Association helped get the players home.'

Friday, December 22, 1989

Last days for a train of thought

The bad news is that one of my great dreams is unlikely to be realised: the famous train known as Canada Number One makes its last journey on the 14th of January next year.

It runs, as you all know, from Montreal to Vancouver, a trek of almost three thousand miles.

And for great measure it touches towns at some stations with marvellous names.

We have all heard of Moose Jaw and Medicine Hat but not everybody knows about Indian River and Swift Current and Locust Hill.

Swift Current is an especially marvellous name.

It sits on the shelf with Gleannsharoon and Kilmainhamwood and Castle Island and Etoile and Melrose and Market Rasen and Portaferry and Lyrecrompane.

Up there too and shining brightly are Montmartre and Newcastlewest and Four Roses and Carmarthen and Passage West and Winchester and Watergrasshill.

And I mustn't forget Portobello and Welshpool and Shrewsbury and Sheharee and Guadalajara and Lookout Mountain and Wounded Knee.

And of course there are Gortacoppal and Clashnagook and Chipping Camden and Montparnesse and Canterbury and Inchicore.

And how could I omit the name of the mountain village which is part of folklore...

Arise Knocknagoshel and take your place among the nations of the earth.

Let us return to the unreal world; I am talking, of course, about Irish rugby.

For a start I must confess that I do not attend those famous training sessions where everything goes according to plan – according to our successive managers.

I attended one a great many years ago – and said "Never again"

I would much prefer to watch something really exciting, such as a concrete mixer at full throttle or men digging holes or women knitting socks – or even cardigans.

And so I wasn't present last Sunday when strange things happened in a field in Dublin Four.

You may not have heard about it – indeed one morning paper more or less ignored it.

At the end of a training stint a mini-match was staged.

The 'official' team contained twelve of those who played recently against the All-Blacks.

The three replacements were no daws; indeed one, Michael Kiernan, would have played against New Zealand but for injury.

This was a mini-match only in that it was played in two halves of twenty minutes each.

At the interval the 'unofficial' side led by an amazing basket of points.

For good measure the side contained only fourteen players.

In the second half the officials were also down to fourteen – but little good it seems to have done them; the avalanche continued.

And in the aftermath a man who passes as Jimmy Davidson (his real name is Walter Mitty Junior) professed to be greatly pleased.

Whether he was pleased with the display of the unofficials wasn't clear; he could hardly have been overjoyed with the display of the officials.

In the meantime I have heard various explanations of the debacle.

We are told that the match was played on the back pitch – I cannot see what great difference that made.

And we are told that the officials weren't trying – indeed...

There are two reasons for suspecting that explanation.

For a start, very few of the officials would be automatic selections for the imminent match with England.

And for a finish, rugby is not a game which you can play 'easily'.

Yes, I know about those exhibitions where the score ends up at something like 57-55. They do not count.

Last Sunday's affair wasn't on exhibition; it was a 'friendly', – and in rugby there are no friendlies.

It may be unwise to dwell on the score-line in the mini-match – and yet it can hardly be ignored.

And it seems to have offered evidence that strengthens a theory I have often uttered here and elsewhere.

It is this: the pool of our potential internationals is far deeper than most gurus tell us.

How often have we heard, especially in bad times, some 'expert' say: "Our pool is very shallow..."

I will forgive the crazy metaphor; I cannot forgive the judgement; I find it insulting and discouraging.

And for bad measure, it is nonsensical – as was proven not too long ago by that post-season expedition to France.

And rugby aficionados in the real world outside Ireland must suspect that we have a very deep pool indeed.

The strange case of Hugo Mac Neill is sufficient proof that some of our selectors are not the full shilling.

When he was just about the best full-back in Rugby Union, he couldn't command a place even on the Leinster team.

I suspect too that those responsible for putting Canada's most famous train into dry dock are less than intelligent.

Canada as a nation is going through its growing pains.

The old joke tells us that all the Canadians have in common is a distrust of The United States.

The Number One train was a great link; it is the falsest of economy to silence it.

The consolation is that the line is not to be taken up.

Our home-grown vandals tore the heart from one of the finest rail systems in the world; at its peak it reached into every nook in this island

– and a great many crannies.

Now we have a skeleton service. And where once we had splendid horizontal ladders, we now see open wounds.

Whenever I think about that monstrous crime against the people, I have doubts about the wisdom of abolishing capital punishment.

And I incline towards an oft-quoted definition of the ideal democracy – "Constitutional government tempered with judicious assassination."

Incidentally, the great railroad from Montreal to Vancouver was built in the 1870s and '80s.

Thirty thousand men worked on it; this was one of the greatest navvying feats of all time.

And it is known in the country's folklore as 'The ribbon of steel.' It is also The National Dream.

Some of our lads were, of course, involved; sadly, a man of Irish descent is involved in its closure; Brian Mulrooney is the current Prime Minister.

The Canadians have a saying for the crime; "Mulrooney has driven the last spike into The National Dream."

———

Tuesday, September 5, 1989

Wembley '66

Of course you have heard it before – but don't stop me: I am talking, of course, about that marvellous day long ago when England played West Germany in the final of The World Cup.

It was the first World Cup to be broadcast on television in this country – we have never been the same since.

I watched every match that was on the box; I saw the rest in my imagination.

And I looked forward to the final like a small boy about to be taken to his first circus.

And on the eve of that momentous event it seemed that my dream would be snatched away.

A kinsman had taken ill and I was requested to draw his turf out of the bog.

And it was with a heavy heart I set out that July morning for the mountain country of Ahaneboy.

Up there I was to make contact with a grand man called Batt Greaney; he would provide the horse and car.

And about half-past seven we arrived at the rectangle where our kinsman's turf was high and dry in stooks.

The night had rained; the bog was rather soft on top; Batt and I inspected the going – and decided that it was too heavy.

I must confess that it was not an objective judgement; I had often ferried out turf in far worse conditions.

And so that day over 23 years ago will go down in history as the only occasion on which I ate a second breakfast.

And it was with a light heart that I went down into the valley and took up my traditional place in one of my favourite pubs.

Strangely enough, it wasn't Paddy Hussey's, even though I had seen much of the tournament there.

I suspected that Paddy's would be all-ticket for the final – and so I adjourned to another pub in The Latin Quarter.

And so it was in Monny McGillicuddy's that I watched what I still consider the second-greatest game of Association Football that I ever saw.

Castle Island is one of the last bastions of civilisation – and, of course, the television set wasn't in the bar.

It was in the living quarters, at the end of a long room that served as parlour and kitchen.

It was crowded, so much so that my old friend, Bertie O'Brien, made a little bit of history.

He knelt down near the box and didn't get up until the game was over.

And I will never forget his summing up: "What will we do for the rest of the year?"

In his own simple way he had said it all; it had been a great tournament and it brought a new dimension into our lives.

And, of course, it hastened the end of the infamous Ban, the epitome of green ignorance and prejudice.

In those far-off and not unhappy days I hadn't the slightest suspicion that I might one day be a journalist.

In truth I am not – but I work for a newspaper.

And, high and behold, in the midsummer of 1982 I found myself on the way to Spain to keep an eye or two on the finals of The World Cup.

On that Sunday evening in Gatwick I was more than somewhat uneasy.

Somebody with a rather quirky sense of humour had made my travel arrangements – and I was billeted in Segovia, over 70 miles from Madrid.

I can never forget that journey up into the mountains; it was a steaming night and the bus had no air conditioning.

And when we arrived at the hotel, our worst fears were confirmed – the bar was as closed as George Bush's mind.

On the journey I had made friends with an Australian – and Harold and I went into action.

We cajoled a young boy to go to the home of the bar manager; he came back with the keys.

It was about three o'clock. Never did beer taste so good.

The people of Spain may have their faults but they make great ale.

Next day we journeyed down to Madrid and passed through country where a cow would have to travel several miles to fill her belly.

The mountains of Castile still haunt me; I would love to go back and walk in that hard brown country, even at the risk of being devoured by wolves – hungry or otherwise.

That Spanish tournament provided some marvellous football; ironically, the best came from Brazil, but they didn't even reach the semi-finals.

Their knock-out game with Italy took place a long way from Madrid; I watched it on television in the company of Eoin Hand and Billy Young.

And we were about equally heartbroken when our favourite team fell out.

One of the shrewdest players in the world was woefully at fault for the fatal goal; Junior was slow to move out after a place-kick had been partly cleared – and put Paolo Rossi onside; the stoat pounced.

Rossi was, of course, the hero of the tournament; it was the Everest of irony; a few months previously he had been convicted of throwing games.

A little while ago I spoke about the second-greatest game of soccer that I ever saw – the greatest was in that Spanish tournament.

I have vivid memories of that glowing morning when Harold and myself flew down to Seville.

I can still visualise the great seas of giant sunflowers that are grown to produce oil.

Seville is a fairly big city – but, believe it or not, when we dropped in to a pub, we met Peter Byrne and Charlie Stuart.

And that night we watched West Germany and France in the semi-final; it was the greatest game of football – any code – that I ever saw.

And, as the world knows, it contained the most outrageous example of injustice ever perpetrated.

I can still see Patrick Battiston speeding down the inside-left channel – and Harald Schumacher moving out to meet him.

The keeper's greeting was not over friendly; in fact, he knocked Patrick unconscious – he was near death when the doctor reached him.

And the keeper wasn't sent off: he wasn't even booked – France didn't even get a free.

West Germany got through by way of the penalty shoot-out – but they were a weary team in the final.

There was a heatwave that summer along the Mediterranean; that night in Seville the temperature was 127.

Italy were much the fresher team on that Sunday night in Madrid; they won going away.

I watched West Germany again in the Mexican finals; there Diego Maradona came between them and the ultimate glory.

Next morning I met several of Franz Beckenbauer's warriors in Mexico City's famous craft shop, The Rio.

They were the saddest men I had encountered since a Monday morning in Mulligan's in the late September of '82.

On that occasion myself and John O'Keeffe decided that the only anodyne was champagne.

Wednesday, February 1, 1995.

Mikey ahead of his time

Perhaps you had better things to do than peer at the picture that showed Rob Andrew on his way through Dublin Airport on the Thursday before the recent big game; he had such a mound of luggage on the trolley that you could barely see his cherubic face. Now read on . . .

What was he doing? Was he leaving home for good? Was he bringing with him all his goods and chattels? Was he perhaps fearful that there was a shortage of food and drink in The Republic? I doubt if any of these speculations has a foundation.

I suspect that most of his luggage consisted of raiment. Your modern player of rugby is not akin to a very fine professional in another code whom I met one Sunday long ago after a game in Glenmalure Park – he had his gear in a brown paper bag.

And why shouldn't he... All he needed were his shorts and his stockings and his boots. His shirt was in the skip. As I had a drink with that modest man, I remembered an almost-forgotten Sunday when I went up to the players' gate in Thomond Park and was asked for my credentials; I produced my shorts from one pocket and my stockings from the other.

Time marches on – and your modern player, no matter in what game or at what level, wouldn't leave home without a track suit in his bag. Perhaps Rob Andrew and his team-mates need several tracksuits to be donned according to the weather.

That picture of England's out-half recalled for me the memory of a dear friend with whom I played many a game of rugby in the wet and windy fields of Munster; we will call him Mikey because that was his name.

For a great many years he was the utility man on our team; he was probably one of the few players in the history of the oval ball who played as wing-threequarter on one Sunday and as hooker on the next.

Kerry people are inclined to exaggeration but, believe me, all that I am about to say is gospel true – I hasten to add that I have some doubts about certain parts of the Testaments.

To watch Mikey preparing for a game, big or small, was an awe-inspiring spectacle; it was a thousand pities that the video camera wasn't available in those long-lost days.

The ceremony began with the divesting of his street clothes; this was not a casual process; my old friend was a snappy dresser before that label was minted and wouldn't throw his garments down on the floor or any-old-where atall.

The next stage was the rubbing; Mikey would be almost as naked "as an ashtree in the moon of May" as some colleague annointed him from shoulders to ankles with a wicked lotion called Wintergreen.

At last the first item of clothing, if you could call it that, was donned; the jockstrap was followed by a blue bathing trunks; next came the shorts; you may think that by now the worst was over – the ritual was only starting.

There was a kind of corset to be donned and laced; in later life I discovered that this was common practice in New Zealand – our Mikey was ahead of his times.

And then came the jersey, produced by my great friend Danny Horan, gentleman and singer and angler, from our modest skip – and Mikey was rejoicing in the beloved colours of Castle Island R.F.C. – red and white and blue, the original colours of The French Republic.

You may now think that the stockings came next: it wasn't that way atall – the ankles had to be strapped; this was a lengthy and complicated process.

At last came the boots, the precious Cotton Oxfords; they were laced with meticulous care and then at real last came the shinpads and the garters.

A mediaeval knight preparing for battle wouldn't have taken as much time and as much care.

There is, alas, an inset in this tale of the robing which is a little sad – it is essentially a tale about disrobing. Now once again, read on . .

On a legendary Sunday when we won the Galwey Foley Cup against all the odds, the bould Mikey was the especial hero: he sealed the game with a brilliant try which I described in this paper many suns and many moons ago.

That try, I fear, went to my friend's head; he was always a prima donna; on the following Sunday he played hard to get – or at least that was how I interpreted it.

He didn't make a public announcement about his unavailability; he merely broke the awful news to our secretary, Tommy Casey, on his way to Mass; Tommy doubled as sacristan and taker of money at the chapel gate.

There was something amiss with Mikey's back; the news spread like teamfire; life went on; the game wasn't postponed; we travelled to Tralee and assembled in The Meadowlands Hotel.

While most of us were colloguing in the foyer, Mikey went upstairs to commence the long process of robing; we followed in due course and began our modest preparations; eventually Tommy Casey arrived and produced a rectangle of white paper.

And he read out the teamsheet; our hero's name wasn't on it – he had been taken at his word about his back; I can still see his face – disbelief gave way to shock and horror and resentment and anger and self-righteousness. He disrobed in a grim silence – he experienced on that day long ago the humiliation and the embarrassment of a groom who comes to the church in all his shining raiment, only to discover that the bride had cried off.

Again life went on; Mikey didn't go to the game; he went to assuage his sorrows in the bar; when we came back, he was rather the worse for a mixture of Paddy and Guinness and I discovered that he had put the blame on me, even though I hadn't had hand, act, or part, not to mention cut, shuffle, or deal in picking the team; I was only the captain. Nevertheless, I was the culprit – it is the story of my life.

And I was challenged to a fistic duel to take place on the next day; of course it was all fantasy. We were all young and lived happily every after – but I still do not know what Rob Andrew was doing with all that baggage.

———

Saturday, July 15, 1989

The day 'The Yank' had the last laugh

Recently I had reason to re-read 'Glenanaar', a book I hadn't opened for almost twenty years – I was delighted to find it so good.

I returned to it with trepidation; I feared that I would find my old enthusiasm displaced; almost twenty years is a long time in any territory.

Much of what Canon Sheehan wrote is remarkably relevant to our times – but we tend to think of his generation as old-fashioned in a way that previous generations were not.

I cannot explain why: perhaps it is because Sheehan's generation is so close that we see in it the roots of our own; in a way it invokes Herbert Read's famous dictum – "The past of every reasonable man is strewn with dead enthusiasms."

Sheehan grew up in Mallow, a town that has long been a hotbed of sport.

In his 'Literary Life And Other Essays' he has a delightful passage about his home town's cricket club.

For several years in his young manhood they were unbeaten – and this was at the highest level by Irish standards.

You may suspect that the game in Mallow was played by only the upper classes – it wasn't that way atall.

It was a game for all classes, just as it was in Francis Ledwidge's young manhood in Meath; the poet tells us how a batsman who had lost his wicket might go to play football in another part of the field.

Sheehan loved hurling too – and the opening chapter in 'Glenanaar' contains an account of a decidedly dramatic county final.

Before we come to that game which figured so much in the old national school readers, we meet a rather mysterious man known locally as The Yank.

He comes to a town which is a cross between Doneraile and Mallow and puts up at the hotel.

His obvious prosperity is the envy of the locals; the older element regret that they didn't emigrate to America; the younger people are determined not to let slip their chance.

Anyhow, when the day of the county final comes, the magnificently-garbed Yank is in the crowd.

Strangely enough, the game is billed as a tournament; Sheehan wryly says –"In past times it used to be called a hurling match, but we are going ahead in Ireland, and we call things now by their proper names.

"At three o'clock the teams are called to their places by the captains. There is a brief consultation with the referee, a coin was flung into the air... and in a moment one could see the ball tossed hither and thither in the struggle – and a confused mass of men and camans as they fought fiercely for victory and the tide of battle rolled uncertain here and there across the field."

Sheehan goes on: "And the contestants were strangely silent. This, too, is a modern characteristic, and a wholesome one. Instead of the whoops and yelps of olden times one saw only the set faces ... of these young athletes as they strained every nerve... for victory."

About ten minutes from the final blow, the local captain is taken ill.

There is consternation in the ranks of the Skirmishers – "Just on the point of victory, their hopes were dashed to the ground."

"They held a long ... consultation and finally decided to enlist one or other of the spectators who was a member of the Club."

This makes you wonder about the substitute position – but let it pass.

Anyhow, the plan is abandoned – the issue is too important. And as the clock approaches five of the hour, the referee threatens to award the match to the city team.

Then comes a moment of high drama: The Yank steps forward, takes off his coat and waistcoat, and takes up a caman, tests it and says – "Let me take a hand; I guess I can manage it."

Needless to say, there is a general laugh; I suspect that you could call it a guffaw.

The Shandons are delighted – they see the grey hairs in hair and beard.

The Skirmishers are less than enthusiastic – but one of them is wiser than the rest; he sees that The Yank is splendidly built – and says "We'll take him, put him right inside the goal."

You will see that he was posted to the back four, though I doubt if that term was at large at the time.

Excitement, already high enough, now o'erleaps itself; some people expect to have the privilege of seeing a man die in battle.

The ball is tossed in again; the battle sways up and down; cheers rise wildly from the two sets of partisans.

The match goes into the last minute – and the city team go all out for the winning goal.

In doing so they drive the ball into the Yank's reach – on the ground, in case you'd like to know.

And the unlikely replacement explodes into action and begins to carve a path through the swaying mass of friends and foes.

"The Yank struck straight before him and with his powerful arms and shoulders cut his way as clean as a swathe of ripe corn is levelled by a mowing machine."

The local partisans went mad, that is if they weren't mad already.

"And the tumult culminated in a wild Irish cheer ... as despite the frantic efforts of the Shandons' keeper, the ball passed out gaily through the gates of the goal."

And just as The Yank struck the winner, a mass of opponents bore down on him and he was flung under a human pile.

He is unable to get up and is borne on a stretcher from the field.

And someone asks him what Sheehan calls a distinctly Gaelic question: "You're not dead are you?"

He wasn't and he advises the ill captain: "You go home, young man, and liquor yourself up as fast as you can."

And a veteran aficionado puts in his spoke: "Begor, there was nothing seen like it since Casey the Hurler's time."

The Yank says: "That was a long time ago, I guess" and leaves it at that.

And you will not be surprised when eventually you find out that The Yank is no less than Terence Casey himself.

It's all great stuff and you can read it for yourself when O'Brien Press republish 'Glenanaar' in a few months time.

Friday, November 17, 1989

Crack 100 in the Dusk

It is always the same; no matter where you are, you feel lonely when you see lights coming on in the distance at nightfall. I remember especially an evening in Mexico City during the World Cup in 1986 when that experience penetrated me in a way I could never forget.

It was after a match in which one of my favourite teams had lost out – that of course didn't help.

Above in the hills behind that grossly overcrowded conurbation the lights were coming on - for some reason beyond the obvious it was one of the saddest moments in my life.

I experienced a similar sadness last Wednesday evening.

The Republic of Ireland had just completed the first leg of their World Cup voyage – and I should have been singing and dancing.

Believe me, I wasn't: of course I was delighted that a dream had come true – and yet I was probably the saddest person in or around Ta'Qali Stadium.

Away to the south-west of that bizarre arena is a world where escarpments of stone predominate.

By comparison Clare's famous Burren is a gentle and friendly place.

You could hardly believe that anyone could live up there – and yet it seems that people do.

When on Wednesday evening I saw the first light there, I thought it came from a passing vehicle.

Soon I saw that it didn't – unless the vehicle was broken down or had picked up a puncture or otherwise been brought to a halt.

Then a second light came on – and soon a third.

And I realised that up in the anti-human world there were people.

All around me there was an ecstasy in green.

The Barleycorn were blasting out The Fields of Athenry; the crack was 100 in the dusk. And yet there was I, alone and palely loitering, like Michael Henchard at his daughter's wedding-feast.

Of course you remember him – he is the hero or anti-hero of Thomas Hardy's most celebrated novel, 'The Mayor of Casterbridge'.

His life went astray – and at what should have been a great occasion for him, he watched from outside a window in the hotel dining-room.

And so now you have a fair idea of how I felt about five o'clock last Wednesday evening.

Of course it was madness on my part but I could do nothing about it.

Instead of rejoicing because the good ship Republic of Ireland had got the clearance for a great voyage, I was like a man in thrall to melancholy.

Instead of worrying about what group we would be given in the finals, I was wondering about those people up in that land of stone where the lonely lights were coming on.

What had they been working at all day? And how would they spend the night?

Would they sit around the fire and talk or play cards or maybe sing the odd song?

Or would they go down to the pub? And, believe me, Malta abounds in lovely pubs.

And, God between us and all harm, would they just watch television?

We are all tormented by the unknown – and this was an occasion worse than most.

Back at home in Kerry I would be lonely too as the lights came on at nightfall, even though I would have a fair idea of the texture of my neighbours' lives.

Jack Mick would be going across the hill to play 31 in Tom Billy's house.

And his wife, Mary Anne, would be at home with a few of her friends making apple jam and talking about knitting patterns.

And, being the time of the year that it is, Micky Joe would be down at the river with his trusty gaff under his coat.

And his good wife might be down below in the glen cooing over her latest grandchild.

And Thady Pat – now you wouldn't be too sure about his whereabouts. That same man is not given to orthodoxy; more than likely he would be distilling a few gallons of malt for the Christmas.

And what about his good wife? You must be joking. Thady has no wife, good, bad or indifferent – I told you that he wasn't given to orthodoxy.

Anyway, you have got the drift of what pass for my ideas.

When you can be lonely at home as the lights come on at nightfall, how do you find a word for such an experience as I suffered last Wednesday evening?

I must confess that there was another reason for my sadness.

We had reached a long-promised land and some great people who had helped mightily to build the ship were not present.

Pat O'Brien has gone to another world. Peadar O'Driscoll and John Farrell were back at home and not in good health.

And what remains of my mind went back to our last match in Malta, on that crazy afternoon when a black wind blew up from Africa and added to the difficulties of a diabolical pitch.

And on Wednesday I missed those absent warriors of that match five-and-a-half years ago; like the present crew, they were a grand lot.

I missed especially those to whom I was close – Liam Brady and Mark Lawrenson and Michael Robinson.

It's a funny old world – and that's for sure.

Do you remember about ten years ago our scenario for the visa to the finals of the World Cup?

Our team would be built around four especial players – David O'Leary and Mark Lawrenson and Liam Brady and Frank Stapleton.

And what happened?

Mark is grounded for life.

Liam seems to have no part in Jack's greenprint.

David is playing brilliantly with club and country – but Our Jack suspects brilliance.

He is certain to be in the expedition for Italy, but more than likely as a bit player.

The same seems true of Frank; John Aldridge and Tony Cascarino are now established.

And what then about Jim Beglin? Don't tell me that luck plays no part in this universe.

Stephen Staunton should count his blessings – he is hardly a wet year on The Republic's team and can now look forward to playing in the World Cup finals.

Wednesday, March 24, 1993

Cheltenham Pilgrimage

Patrick Kavanagh for once was wrong when he denounced the Irish love of the horse as a myth.

He himself was a contradiction of that statement; few people have been more devoted to the betting shop.

Perhaps that devotion owed more to the gambling instinct than to a love of horses; I suspect that it owed something to both.

The institution known as The Cheltenham Festival is a rare phenomenon in that the Irish give the impression that they outnumber the British there.

Of course they do not, but their propensity for not keeping their light under a bushel or even a Bushmills might convince someone from the outside world that he had discovered an Irish colony in Britain.

Soon we will experience another example of our preoccupation with the noble animal.

On the Saturday of The Grand National a time will come about midway through the afternoon when the Martians could take over the country without firing a shot or aiming a ray gun.

And if they could find someone and ask him to take them to our leader, it might be a question without an answer.

I need hardly explain; it is almost certain that our leader would be at the great race.

Perhaps The Grand National evokes a similar madness in the neighbouring island – but I doubt it.

Before I was sent into exile, I was the local amanuensis – unpaid, I hasten to add.

And on Grand National day, I used to take up my post in a pub adjacent to our local betting shop.

It was Myra McCarthy's, in case you wish to know; her son-in-law, John Shanahan, is now on the bridge.

And for hours before the race there would be a flow of clients; most of my neighbours could read but few had any practice in the skill of writing.

I transmuted their forecasts into script – it was all great crack.

And in those innocent years I came upon an unwritten rule.

It is this: if a horse came home at even 500/1, you could be certain that somebody would have backed him or her.

And you could be certain that you would get currency notes that might be out of circulation

Someday someone will write a thesis about the significance of the biscuit tin in rural Irish culture.

I grew up in a world where the horse was king.

The tractor had yet to come; horse power – not to mention donkey power – was a mighty element in the economy.

Our family hadn't much in the way of broad acres – indeed all we had were a few very narrow acres – but we had a horse.

She was a half-bred mare; my old man bought her in a moment of madness.

He brought her home about midnight from the local fair and, believe it or not, insisted on bringing her into the wee room where I was sleeping.

She was then a three-year-old – she lived to be thirty-nine; that, for a horse, is an incredible age.

Country people have an unshakeable belief in what they call breeding.

In the context of horses they have an ancient saying: "You can't bate the blood."

This means that horses with a tincture of Arabian breeding have bottomless courage.

And the belief is well founded.

In Canon Sheehan's great book, Glenanaar, there is a little story which exemplifies this.

A curate has a half-bred mare to whom he is devoted so much that he would never touch her with a whip.

One night he is going on a sick call, so urgent that for the first time ever he gives the mare a touch of the whip.

She runs her heart out – literally.

When he reaches the house, he gives the mare to the husband to tie her up.

Then he goes to the trough to wash his hands; the man of the house follows him – and says: "She is dead." And the priest says: "Your wife?" and the man says: "No, your mare."

And the priest is relieved; he has come in time to give Extreme Unction.

That little story tells a lot about horses and about the priesthood.

I need hardly add that the connection between Irish priests and racing is a salient part of our culture.

Our old friend, Father Sean Breen, is the most famous clerical aficionado of the racing game.

He figured in a great double last week; he starred in articles in The Sporting Life and in The Guardian.

Michael Clower did the piece in The Life; my dear friend, Cynthia Bateman, was the interviewer in The Guardian.

They were great pieces – and put out flags for the priesthood, especially the Irish species.

Sean is from Cavan; nevertheless, he is a good and a holy man.

I loved his answer when asked why he wears layman's clothes at the races.

"Does a surgeon go in his white coat or a nurse in her uniform?" Indeed . . .

Sean has been going to Cheltenham for about twenty-five years – it is his annual pilgrimage.

I might as well add that being from Cavan isn't his only affliction – he also follows Manchester United.

I have been going to Cheltenham for as long as I care to remember.

It is a strange town – at least to us Irish; it is so laundered that if you dropped a bus ticket, you would go back to pick it up.

I had long thought that Cheltenham was a kind of promised land – one day I discovered otherwise.

It was the first day of The Festival; I was up from London and had a few hours to spare.

I decided to do a little bit of research away from the town centre and the main streets.

And I discovered pubs where the clients were palpably not overburdened with worldly wealth.

If you ever make the journey from London to Cheltenham, you will pass through lovely country.

Most of us are familiar with The Thames Valley but perhaps not with the world between Swindon and The Cotswolds.

It is enchanting country – valleyed and wooded and watered.

And it has towns that are encrusted by time – Stroud and Kemble and Stonehouse.

Usually nowayears I stay in Birmingham – I miss that voyage through the past.

My favourite story about The Cheltenham Festival is so bizarre that it has to be true.

It is set on a Gold Cup day; the publicans are coming up from London on an almighty freebie.

About half-way to The Holy Land a man comes along the train saying rather loudly; "Is there a Catholic priest on board?"

And a voice pipes up: "Has somebody become ill?" "No – we're looking for a bottle opener."

———

Monday, October 2, 1989

Nissaning to spoken music

I know who invented the steam-engine, the aeroplane, the safety pin, the washing board, the non-stick frying pan, the combustion engine, and the modern sliotar – but not, strangely enough, the bicycle.

It is a woefully deep flaw in my armour. The bicycle in its own quiet and humble way has changed the world so much that you could legitimately talk of the pre-bicycle age and the bicycle age.

And you could also borrow a few words from poetry and refer to it as a thing of beauty and a joy forever.

A generation ago, or perhaps two, in this country you could hear grown men and ungrown men arguing furiously about the virtues of various makes, so much so that a visitor who didn't know the language might have thought that they were arguing about their horses.

In my youthful fantasies I believed that you could judge a man by his bike.

The solid citizen – let him be a big farmer or a publican or a merchant – favoured the Rudge; the common man preferred the Raleigh; the yuppie – as yet unchristened – went for the B.S.A. or the Royal Enfield.

And of course the super-yuppie went in for the low-slung handlebars; he mightn't be a racing cyclist but at least he could look like one.

And of course the gearcase was a powerful symbol; it was the mark of the conservative, the man who carries a raincoat even when the forecast is for dry weather and who would never forget his bicycle clips.

In those distant days we had heard about The Tour of France but it seemed to belong to a world that we would never inhabit.

Then came the first of the stage races – and great was the excitement along the route.

It was as if the outside world had come to us; we were getting a taste of the continent.

Men from far off the main roads - men whom normally you would see only on Sundays or fair days or at Duffy's Circus - came from their fastnesses to wait and watch.

People used to take up their positions long before the expected time; rumours inevitably came along, some of them more or less true; then would come the first signs that the cavalcade was imminent.

First came the outriders on motor-bikes; then came the official cars; then after a little interval that seemed a sample of eternity, the leading riders appeared; soon came the bunch – we have a different name for it now.

And then the flood began to fall until a stream of stragglers came by - and inevitably a few came when only the most dedicated remained to see.

I well remember the first C.R.E. race; the Killarney-Limerick stage went by our house; I can still clearly see Shay Elliott wearing the yellow jersey and well ahead of the pack as he powered up the four-mile hill that peaks a little beyond Gleannsharoon.

Shay was to become our great pioneer on the continent; he would never win The Tour but did well enough in it to prove that the continentals were not a different species.

Sean Kelly prospered on that knowledge; Stephen Roche reaped the harvest sown by Shay Elliott.

The experts tell me that Kelly is a member of a long tradition; the typical tour cyclist is a country boy, one who takes hours of hard toil for granted.

Seemingly that was the pattern on the continent until recent years; Stephen Roche is perhaps one of a new breed.

It was good to see him back this week, working quietly towards rehabilitation.

And it was good to see the infant Nissan Classic growing up so sturdily.

O'Connell Street was the capital of the cycling world for about an hour yesterday afternoon.

By four a mass of humanity crowded against the barriers even though it was well known that the race was behind schedule.

Multi-coloured cars bristling with advertisements lined the quays.

The O'Connell monument was festooned with small boys.

An exceedingly agile youth had shinned up a light standard on the bridge - I suppose you could call it the pole position.

The tannoy kept the crowd well informed; it was clear that the Irish riders wouldn't win the over-all – but that didn't seem to take from the excitement.

The harbingers were the same as ever; I might have been back on a hillside in Kerry a generation ago, only that the motor-bikes were a different breed.

Then came the company cars; the word 'Nissan' proliferated.

I was watching the toll bridge away on the horizon; there the passing cars seemed like toys.

I would like to say that I discerned the first bunch of riders as they crossed it - but I didn't.

And when they came along Eden Quay, they were so close together and travelling at such a clip that I couldn't pick out one that I could name - they might as well have been starlings.

When the first flurry of excitement had passed, I went down to the traffic island near the junction of the quay and Butt Bridge.

And when the next bunch came, I could hear the song of the spokes.

And I was near enough to see the expressions - and once again my heart went out to those great and brave men.

In Mulligan's famous back room I watched most of the round-the-city-centre finish.

The camera we are told doesn't lie - but in the soft light of autumn our capital city looked almost continental.

And I rode in my imagination those last few miles with Phil Anderson; because he was so bold, I didn't wish to see him caught.

With his big-boned unshaven face and his dark hair streaming behind him, he was one of the few that you could easily recognise.

At the line he couldn't have got a greater reception if he had been one of our own.

I went up to the G.P.O. to see some of the folk heroes in the flesh.

I spotted Charlie Mottet but hardly in the flesh, more in the skin and bone.

This little man from The Alps is more like a jockey than a racing cyclist

– but then of course they are jockeys in their own way.

Eric Vanderaerden looks a member of a different species; the overall winner is a blonde powerful Belgian; his winning of four stages in a row was a mighty feat.

I met a man in the Fagor colours - and I asked him if he had been in the race.

"Only" he said "as a mechanic". And I said to myself; "Why the 'only'?"

Do you remember the brothers Orville and Wilbur Wright who lived long ago in Dayton, Ohio? They were bicycle mechanics - in their spare time they invented the aeroplane.

Friday, April 14, 1989

Exploring the hidden Lancashire

Last Saturday morning I travelled from Manchester Airport to Liverpool in a chauffeur-driven Mercedes, accompanied by a senior member of our Cabinet and a lady trainer and a jockey – my return journey was a little more modest.

I wouldn't have been in any hurry home but for the Cavan-Dublin game in Croke Park – and so I was booked on the eight o'clock flight out of Manchester.

I left Aintree after the fourth race, got back to Liverpool by train and disembarked at Central Station.

That same station deserves no marks for organisation; I didn't mind it being dreary – but I searched in vain for a destination board.

I asked two of the staff about trains for Manchester: they were pleasant – but their information was contradictory.

I had visions of ending up in Preston or Carlisle or maybe over the border in Scotland itself – or maybe down below in Plymouth or even Dorchester.

And so I decided to go over to The Adelphi and get a taxi; I had won a few pounds on Feroda and Cloughtaney and was in a mildly expansive mood.

I didn't get to that famous hotel; on the way I passed close to Cable

Street bus station and spotted a vehicle headlined "MANCHESTER".

It was unmanned and empty but near the door there was a resolute-looking woman complete with shopping-bags; departure was imminent.

On both sides of the bus in big letters was a notice saying "EXPRESS"; the omens were good – I would be in Manchester with at least an hour and a half to spare.

In my vision the bus would get quickly out of Saturday-evening Liverpool and onto the M62 and reach Manchester in about an hour.

Little did I know – I was about to embark on a tour of South Lancashire's by-ways.

The driver, a big man with a fine easy presence, duly arrived; the fare was so low – £1.60 – that it should have alerted me.

If this bus was an express, the word had taken on a new meaning; it halted at every stop – and stops are frequent in South Lancashsire.

That wouldn't have mattered so much if so many of the passengers weren't old and dear friends of the pilot.

In both their comings and their goings they stopped for long chats with him – obviously he is a kind of quiet local hero.

The bus left Cable Street a little after five; at half-past the hour it was still in Liverpool; my scenario was awry.

By now it was dawning on me that the M62 was not on; this bus was meant to pick up passengers all along the route.

And suddenly Manchester Airport seemed a very long distance away.

I started doing my sums; at the rate we were going – or not going – we wouldn't reach the centre of Manchester until about half-past seven.

And the airport is about eight miles from the city. The sweat began to break out.

Nevertheless, the bus kept on in its oft-interrupted way, travelling through or near towns with names familiar from Rugby League – St. Helens, Wigan, and Swinton.

As we were approaching a rural pub near the village of Lowton, a man hurried down from the upper deck and whispered a few words to the driver.

The bus came to a halt; the man dashed into the pub; he was away about ten minutes – I suspect he wasn't all that time in the washroom.

At the next crossroads there was another considerable delay; a man carrying a square-faced shovel in a plastic bag came on board; obviously he and the driver were blood brothers.

There was another heart-to-heart talk as he disembarked a few miles later. I had no blame to the driver. What could he do? Obviously he was very popular – and he was an excellent pilot.

Now if all this happened here at home, you could be sure that English visitors would say: "How very Irish..."

In other circumstances I would have enjoyed the odyssey: we were passing through lovely countryside, adorned by our neighbours' great passion for trees.

When our vehicle drew into Leigh Bus Station, I was convinced that I was going to lose out; it was at the end of a little queue of buses on a very narrow road. Within ten minutes, however, they all moved off; the prospects were brightening – but victory was still far from certain.

At last a familiar environ hove into view; the outskirts of Salford are not particularly beautiful – but I might have come to The Promised City.

Soon we were in central Manchester; the alleged express deposited its few remaining passengers at Arndale Bus Station.

It was now almost seven. One worry remained. It is not a good time for taxis – Englishmen like to have their regular meals.

I hurried to the nearest rank, across the little park from The Portland Hotel; all worry vanished – a young Pakistani bore me swiftly to Wythenshaw; I had checked in by 25 past seven.

And there was time for a little celebratory drink with some of Feroda's connections. Racing people may have their own ethos but they are excellent company.

———

Wednesday, July 19, 1989

On your bike

Someday someone somewhere will write a thesis on the bicycle; if I had the time, I'd do it myself – maybe when the blackberries have been gathered in, I'll settle down to it.

Just think of the potential for a mighty book: the effect of the bike on courtship patterns alone is raw material for a thesis.

Women's magazines and romantic novels tend to postulate that somewhere in this world everyone has his or her true love; it is a rather mystical belief – but the coming of the bicycle gave it a little more credence.

And the bike is one of the few major inventions that didn't cause unemployment; indeed by greatly increasing the mobility of the workforce it helped to alleviate unemployment – a man out of work in, for example, Castle Island might get a job in Tralee.

And unlike the motor car it doesn't emit carbon dioxide – or whatever it is – and so could be used as a logo for The Green Party.

And of course it doesn't depend on imported fuel – or any kind of fuel; occasionally you must lubricate its moving parts – but the amount of grease and oil needed for every bike in this state in any given year is unlikely to have much effect on the balance of payments.

And this humble mode of conveyance has generated a multitude of stories, some of which are true.

I love especially the one about John Millington Synge; it is set in the island called Aranmore.

He was staying in a cottage on the side of a steep hill; on his first evening there he went down to a pub near the bottom.

He came out at some godly hour and wheeled a bike up the boreen; he was aware that someone was walking a little distance behind him – but he was too busy putting words together in his head to take much notice.

Eventually, as you have probably guessed, he reached the cottage – and just as he was about to open the door, a man came up to him and said gently: "Mr. Synge, if it isn't any inconvenience to you, I'll need that bike to-morrow."

And of course there is the oft-told tale about A.E. and the man whose firm manufacture explosives but give munificent awards for people who propagate peace.

The visiting Scandinavian was at a party at the sage's house in Rathgar; when it came to home time, it was too late to get a taxi.

And so AE got out the oul' bike – a Rudge with 28 inch wheels and a three-speed gear, in case you'd like to know – and they bore off gallantly towards The Shelbourne.

Nothing untoward happened until they were crossing Portobello Bridge; there a burly (weren't they all...) constable halted them and said: "In the name of God, Mr. Russell, where are you going with Nobel on your bike?"

And I love – although I shouldn't – the one about the wee man who one day long ago purchased a bicycle in his native Aberdeen.

The machine was wheeled out; the wee man paid cash and got his receipt but remained at the counter; eventually the perplexed clerk said: "Are you waiting for something?" – and the wee man said: "The free wheel."

And of course you all know the one about Patrick Keeffe, the greatest of all the Sliabh Luachra fiddle players.

"Last Sunday I went back to the pub about nightfall and left my bike outside against the wall; when I came out, the wall was there but the bike was gone."

Now stop me if you have heard the next one: it isn't really a story atall – but nevertheless we'll press on.

It concerns my father, God rest him, a man who though completely untrained had a fair knowledge of machines and all their works and pomps.

My colleague and sometimes friend, Michael Cronin, will bear me out when I say that there was a time when the biggest name in the bicycle world was Brady's of Clonmel.

And like Cotts' of Kilcock they did a lot of their business by post.

My old man could write but he believed the I could write better – and for a long time he kept asking me to send a letter to the good people in Clonmel.

I knew the da even better then he knew himself and I kept putting back the concoction of the epistle in the hope that he might forget all about it.

He didn't; indeed as time went by, the request intensified – and an innocent bystander might think that the letter to Brady's would be the key to the promised land.

Eventually the letter was composed and despatched; in three days – believe it or not – a bulky envelope was delivered to our humble abode.

It contained a catalogue outlining the virtues of a wide range of bicycles.

The da was now as happy as a pig rooting for acorns as he revelled in a world of ball-bearings and sprockets and spindles, not to mention springs and brakes and chains and free wheels.

Time went by; there was no request to write a letter; the 'Open Sesame' seemed to have been forgotten.

And then a letter came bearing the Clonmel postmark.

In as courteous a manner as you could expect from a bicycle dealer it outlined a list of extras that would be added.

They included a gear-case, a spare pump, and a carbide lamp.

More time went by – and then one day another missive arrived from the capital of Tipperary's South Riding.

It contained a list of more extras, including a complete tool-kit, an oil pump, and a basket that could be attached to the handlebars.

The da remained unmoved; we heard no more from Brady's of Clonmel – obviously the good people knew a non-runner when they encountered one.

I felt a bit guilty about it all.

This recent weekend I enjoyed a rare experience – a Sunday at home; almost certainly if will be the last such one this year.

I enjoyed tremendously the broadcast of The Tour.

In case you didn't know, Sunday's stage was a time trial, what the French call the trial of truth – because every rider has to perform without the help of domestiques.

This trial was mostly uphill, indeed upmountain – and thus provided a great spectacle for the huge crowds that lined every yard of the road.

The good people of the Lower Alps were marvellous; of course they gave especial applause to their fellow-countrymen – but they encouraged everyone.

And up these heavy gradients the riders needed every whit of encouragement they could get.

The Tour of France is just about the most harrowing examination known to sporting man; without the enthusiasm of the spectators it would be unendurable.

And of course Sean Kelly's performance was a great bonus for all of us who were watching.

And it demolished another myth: for years we have been listening to the experts telling us that Sean cannot climb.

And, lo and behold, Sean went up that mountain road even more powerfully than Pedro Delgado himself.

He may never win cycling's greatest prize but Sean Kelly will figure large when the history of the modern Tour is composed.

It was long believed that the tour was a race for peasants – because only men used to long days in the fields could endure it.

In recent years it has been won by men who wouldn't know a mangold from a turnip – but such as Kelly and Delgado remind us of the old belief.

That's all another story; for anyone who completes the tour – whether he is a townie or a culchie – I have enormous admiration.

The Hurling and Football Annual 1998

The Glory days return for Kerry

It was all so different when I lived in Kerry: whoever said that absence makes the heart grow fonder was spot on; I realised the truth of this one-liner in the run-up to the All-Ireland Final of 1975. For better or worse, I was then living in Dublin. The game took on a deeper emotional involvement for me than when I was living down at home.

On the morning of the battle I didn't partake of a hearty breakfast - indeed I hadn't a breakfast atall. It was a strange occasion: for once Kerry were the outsiders; they had a very young untested team - you could back them at 5/4. Dublin were reigning champions and had performed so well on the way to the title that there was enormous confidence behind them.

A colleague of mine who was a printer in Burgh Quay lost the run of himself on the Saturday night at Shelbourne Park - he put the holiday money on Dublin; in the aftermath his good wife wasn't too pleased. They wouldn't be going to the sun; they spent the holidays in Donabate. A wicked colleague said: "It wasn't the Canaries, it was the Seagulls."

I have very vivid memories of the prologue to the All Ireland Final of 1978. Dublin were even stronger favourites than in 1975. It made sense: they had beaten Kerry convincingly in the Final in 1976 and more so in the semi-final in 1977.

We were very apprehensive. About five o'clock on the Friday evening before the game, the bell rang in my house; outside there was a great friend of mine with his little post office van - what was surely the shortest conversation of all time took place.

Frank Wynne, who has long since departed this world, said, " Well" ....and I said "We'll win." He got into his van and drove away - I was embarrassed that he had such faith in me; well, we won.

At the risk of being barred from my native county, I will argue that Kerry had luck riding shotgun for them on this year's voyage to Autumn Gold.

We didn't encounter the forces we feared most: Clare took out Cork; Cavan eliminated Derry; Meath put out Dublin and were in turn knocked out be Offaly. We didn't fear Mayo because we believed that they were spiritually exhausted - we were wrong there.

Now let us look at the semi-final. Don't tell me that we beat Cavan easily. It's fine to boast that you hadn't feared the storm when you are safe in port. I didn't breathe easily until Miko Russell's goal a few minutes from the end.

About five minutes before, I was convinced that Cavan should have had a penalty; if converted, it would have put them ahead - and only the gods could tell what would happen after that.

The late stages of the final were remarkably similar: we were hanging on by the proverbial thread until Maurice Fitzgerald launched that great point from his hands in the 69th minute - then I knew that we would get at least a draw.

I didn't celebrate that night: I was more relieved than overjoyed - and I remembered a story told by the late John Rafferty, the great sportswriter who doubled as a boxing manager.

His greatest moment came when Jackie Paterson won the World Flyweight Championship. There was only one version of the title then - it was a great achievement. John had guided Jackie from boyhood; it was a night of wild celebration in Glasgow.

What did John do after the fight? He went straight home to bed.

Many people have argued that this year's final was mediocre - I couldn't agree less. The texture was uneven: it was a patchwork quilt of a game that contained many bright colours. Above all, it was sporting - "and for this relief, much thanks." For once, a final left little room for controversy.

It will be remembered as Maurice Fitzgerald's final; he has been so long playing with Kerry that we had almost forgotten it was his first. He had often been accused of under performing but he certainly picked the right day to display all his talents.

There was a belief down in Kerry that Maurice would never win an All-Ireland medal - and as time went by, that belief grew; it was especially strong after last year's semi-final.

The litany of great players who didn't win Gold is very impressive and rather sad - it includes two Kerrymen, Eddie Dowling and my friend, Denis O'Sullivan - they just came along at the wrong time. Count in Gerry O'Malley and Packie Mc Garty and Moses Coffey. Moses was hardly known outside Wicklow but, believe me, he was cast in a heroic mould.

The gods may have smiled on Kerry on their way to winning the All-Ireland but there can be no question about their all-round supremacy in 1997 - they won The League in brilliant style.

The final of that fairer competition provided me with the best day in the sporting year: I was down at the fence behind the City goal about halfway between the posts and the right-hand corner flag. Now read on..... It was raining heavily but I didn't mind: by the 50th minute I knew that Kerry were going to win; the rest of the game was like a lap of honour - I was as happy as a child in sand.

―――

Thursday, June 3 1993

Michael Rides To Glory

Stansted Airport is an acquired taste; yesterday morning I hated it at first sight – it seemed the last place that man ever made.

I remember the time it was first mooted and how fiercely the people of the region fought against the concept.

To me at first acquaintance it seemed a monstrosity of steel and glass, designed by some fiend who abhorred people and wished to make them feel insignificant.

And as I waited in a subterranean limbo for the train to London, I half-believed that I knew how the first space invaders felt when they landed on the moon.

I at least had The Irish Press and could read about Wexford's mental approach to their game against Dublin on Sunday.

The Stansted Express duly arrived from London and soon, as a good shuttle should, headed off west again.

London's third airport was built on marshland; among the objections was the belief that it would wreak havoc with a marvellous tract of natural life.

Perhaps it did but between the airport and London there is a promised land for the lover of nature.

It abounds in splendid ponds where the marshes have been drained; it is like a tabloid version of the Norfolk Broads.

Of course the swans and the mallard are there in glorious numbers; I also saw geese, not all of which I could identify.

This is a strange countryside; it reminds you that Holland isn't very far away – there too the water is king and man is constantly battling against it.

After about three quarters of an hour you reach London with a suddenness that is almost startling.

The approaches to the great city from north and south and west prepare you for a conurbation; the approach from the east is almost surreal.

At one moment you are in deepest country – next you are in Clapton and soon you are speeding through Hackney and Bethnal Green.

Harold Pinter is a native of these parts and expressed the dramatic contrast in a famous phrase – "The weasel in the cocktail cabinet".

Liverpool Street station is not in the Premier League; you never hear it mentioned in the same bracket as Waterloo and Victoria and Charing Cross – and yet I love it.

The marvellous glass dome covers a multitude of flaws; yesterday morning it was teeming – all of human life was there.

It was teeming outside too – it was hardly an occasion for hailing a cab as the hero used to do in the romantic novels of long ago.

And so I took the underground to The Embankment and thence to Waterloo.

It was too early to go to Epsom; the occasion called for a few pints of Murphy in The Hole In The Wall.

It is a plain pub, famous because it is near the entry to a great station.

There was a time when you could see the alleged Great Train Robber, Buster Edwards, having a quiet drink there – and without a cover charge.

He used to sell flowers across the road – now he seems to have retired.

The little pub was very quiet yesterday; there was a group of three; the rest of the drinkers were alone.

The little group were not horny-handed sons of toil; they were commuters – and they spoke commuters' language.

They were near me up at the counter; I couldn't help overhearing – their main theme was the coming of The Channel Tunnel and the effect it would have on their lives.

They were apprehensive but in a muted way as only the English can be.

They are a marvellous people; their genius for ignoring what is outside their own world is enviable.

There now were three intelligent and educated men – and in the hour or so I was in their vicinity they didn't mention The Derby or the imminent game in Oslo.

Soon it was time to head off through leafy South London; it had been a wet spring – and nature is flourishing at its most verdant.

It was raining and so I missed the usual sight of men gardening or playing cricket or tennis, magnificently oblivious of the great race about to unfold nearby.

You shouldn't be surprised. Didn't Francis Drake play bowls as The Armada sailed up The Channel....

It was grey but sultry on The Downs; great white clouds hung ominously.

It had rained there too but the chalky soil was as hard as ever – and the buttercups as tiny.

About half-an-hour before the off in the big race we experienced a familiar sight; the robber barons and their molls strolled down from the parade ring towards the stand.

The Queen came late in the procession; she wore a flat white hat and a blue costume. She is suffering another annus horribilis but she is bearing up.

This year's Derby had a strange start; it took the crowd by surprise.

The announcement about the white flag being up was hardly complete when the horses sprang from the stalls – the usual crazy tumult of shouting was muted.

It was a fairly good start and must have been balm to Keith Brown.

By half-way it was clear that a romantic dream would not come true; Lester Piggott and Fatherland were lost in the pack.

Barathea seemed ideally placed at half-way; Michael Roberts seemed to be holding him up.

As the leading group, including favourite Tenby, lost steam, Michael Kinane must have known that he had a mighty chance.

Commander In Chief was the only proven stayer in the race; he kept on going away and away.

And so Michael achieved a lifetime's ambition – it couldn't happen to a nicer man.

Wednesday, September 13, 1989

An age of innocence and hope

I suppose all of us who attempted to grow up in the thirties have a symbol that brings back the period with especial poignancy. Above all for me it is the rainbow-coloured patches made by a few drops of paraffin oil spilled on a wet metalled road by someone on the way back from the shop.

I do not understand why this should be; perhaps it has something to do with the institution known as the country shop, very much a part of an age when travel was by foot or bicycle or horse.

In those rural emporiums you never had the slightest difficulty in getting any of those little things that seem trivial but without which you could hardly carry on.

Where, for instance, in the city of Dublin today could you readily buy a pair of laces?

And let us suppose you needed that multi-purpose penknife which wouldn't be complete without an instrument for extracting pebbles and grit from horses' hooves…

And is carrageen moss a part of the semi-forgotten past? And has custard made its last stand?

The nineteen-thirties in Ireland is seen by many as a dark age but there were little splinks of light at the end of the tunnel – if only you could find the tunnel.

Those splinks were generated by an abiding sense of hope – and that in turn was generated by an abiding innocence.

About three-quarters of the island had its first native and democratic government; the hardships and the difficulties that abounded were ascribed to the growing pains of the young state.

And of course there was the passionate political partisanship that made even the poorest and the humblest feel part of a tribe that had a roof over its head.

And such was the innocence of the age that every tribe was convinced that it had a monopoly of wisdom and goodness.

Incidentally, it is perhaps a consolation that in this aspect we haven't changed much.

An aspect of this tribal passion was the hunger for leaders who would be seen to stand high above their fellows.

This manifested itself in many fields, most obviously in politics and in sport.

And though there have been great changes since the nineteen-thirties, the hunger for sporting heroes remains.

'Remains' is not, perhaps, the best word; in the meantime the graph of our sporting passion didn't remain constant.

Twenty years ago, for instance, the interest in the All-Ireland finals was not nearly as wide and as deep as it is now.

Of course the crowds flocked to Croke Park on the big days – because the finals are as much social as sporting events; the mental and emotional ambiences, however, were far less.

The return of the 'thirties' atmosphere is, I suspect, a reflection of the times: it is a search for something that is both surrogate and anodyne – even more than half-a-century ago we are in a desert.

In the thirties we could echo Thomas Wolfe's "We are lost but we will be found" – now we are less confident.

I still look back in wonder at those days when a great many people in this island were confident that Jack Doyle would go on and become Heavyweight Champion of the World – that is a fair barometer of the thirties.

Jack himself knew better; his heart was never in the game; he went along with the tide until reality caught up.

Nevertheless, he was delighted one morning about twenty years ago when over a few drinks in my home town, I told him about the excitement he engendered amongst us in his heyday.

Wireless sets were very few then in rural Ireland; telephones were unknown; the men coming home from the creamery brought the papers; people waited eagerly for news of Jack's fight on the night before.

He got great coverage in the infant Irish Press; it was very much a boxing paper, probably due to Joe Sherwood's involvement.

And of course it was a great era for Ireland in the amateur ring, a gold-and-silver age.

I can still visualise the famous faces of the day, not from having seen them in the flesh but in photographs in the papers.

Many of our heroes then were people we would never see in action; we knew them only at second hand but the imagination compensated – sometimes it did more than that.

The interest in boxing was enormous; fights for the world heavyweight championship were anticipated as much as an All-Ireland final.

And below in Kerry we were proud that we had some outstanding amateurs, including one* who went all the way and took a national senior title in the year that World War Two broke out.

And yet, strangely enough, my especial heroes were sons of Dublin – Jimmy Ingle and Paddy Hughes.

I find it hard to explain why, just as people in this island can become passionate supporters of some cross-channel football club without any reason known to themselves.

In the case of Jimmy and Paddy I could hazard a guess – but it is no more that that.

It may have been something in their faces: most pugilists tend to adopt an aggressive expression when posing for a picture – Jimmy and Paddy didn't.

Eventually I was to meet Jimmy – and found that the word 'gentleman' could have been minted for him.

That meeting came about by arrangement; I was to review his autobiography.

I happened to meet Paddy Hughes in very different circumstances. Now read on.

In those days long ago when I used to rush home from school to read The Irish Press, I hadn't the wildest hope that I would ever be a member of the village where it lives.

To me such stars as Joe Sherwood and Roddy The Rover and Anna Kelly and Patricia Lynch dwelt in a different firmament.

Life is like football, it's a funny old business – and by a bizarre series of coincidences I found myself a toiler in Burgh Quay.

And eventually I found myself paying regular visits to the caseroom in The Irish Press building; the purpose was to combat the gremlins that can make a meticulously-crafted piece of prose seem like the ravings of a madman.

This was in the era when most papers were put together by a process

155

known in the trade as 'the hot metal'.

Modern technology has rendered the term 'caseroom' obsolete – its counterpart now is as demure as a convent parlour and about as clangorous as a suburban chemist's shop.

The old caseroom gave you a fair idea of what it was like to work in the boiler room of a tramp ship.

Words battled with the noise – and they weren't all polite.

And it was the rare day that you wouldn't experience a ferocious slanging match between Nicky Rossiter and Jacky Hoban, two bogey-men – their task was to ferry the metal pages on a trolley to the point whence they went down to be printed.

It was all of course an act: Nicky and Jacky were as close as Hamlet and Horatio.

In the midst of all this chaos there was a smallish, neatly-built, bespectacled man who went around cleaning and sweeping and tidying up with all the serenity of a Cistercian monk.

He moved with an ease which hinted that he had been an athlete or a sportsman of some kind – and there was something about his face that made me feel I had known him somewhere sometime.

I couldn't locate the memory – until one day over a few drinks in Mulligan's I sought help from The Irish Press blacksmith, Jimmy O'Connor, God rest him, and he said: "I thought everyone knew Paddy Hughes."

* Oliver Browne

Foreword to Brendan Fullam's book*

Innocent people such as myself like to speculate about pre-history, about the world of which we have no records. When we speak about the 'dawn of history', we mean more or less the time when records began to be kept.

I have a theory concerning the ball-and-stick games that were part of our ancestors' culture – it may be no more than fantasy but I will give it to you.

Early man was a gatherer and a hunter; his hunting was done with his bare hands for a long time. Thus he caught fish and birds and little animals. The next step came when he learned to use missiles, such as rounded stones. Then came a great leap forward in evolution when he began to use tools and weapons. I wasn't around then but I can see my ancestors using a stick to drive rounded stones at flocks and herds.

Man learned to draw before he learned to write; there is an an abundance of depictions to show that ball-and-stick games were widespread in early civilisation.

Hurling was well established in pre-Christian Ireland. In the Brehon Laws you will find sophisticated provisions to compensate the families of any man killed by a hurley or a hurling ball. King Cahir The Great of Tailteann left 50 brass hurleys and 50 brass hurling balls in his will.

There were two forms of hurling in Ireland: winter hurling was played with a narrow stick and a hard ball; summer hurling was played with a broad-bladed stick and a soft ball. You weren't allowed to handle the ball in the former; it was very much a feature of the latter.

Michael Cusack pondered long and deeply when the time came to decide which version he would make official; he chose the summer version, probably because it was more widespread at the time and was more attractive.

Winter hurling survived in the odd nook and occasional cranny; it was played in South-West Kerry until about forty years ago, mainly on the roads and with improvised camáns. It is probably fair to say that summer hurling was played in the better land and by the better-off people – the winter game was favoured more by the working class.

It was played too in our part of Kerry, a few miles north of Castle Island. There was little traffic in the War years; we engaged in fierce battles on the Dublin Road – for a ball we used the bottom half of a small polish box.

Many years later I was delighted to discover that we had been playing winter hurling, much as the two men in one of Moliére's plays were thrilled when they found out that they had been speaking prose all their lives.

When Cusack wrote that the GAA swept the country like a prairie fire, he was thinking mainly of Gaelic football; it proliferated phenomenally. Hurling is our national game in that it is old and unique to us – Gaelic football is the more widespread.

The bogey of tradition has hindered the growth of hurling; there is a mystique about the game that inhibits the so-called lesser counties. We are almost given to believe that every boy in Kilkenny and Cork and Tipperary is born with a wee hurley in one hand and a tiny sliotar in the other; no other county can attain their expertise – so we are told.

In this generation we have seen the ancient game make some progress. A big factor was the emergence of The Faithful County in 1981. The emergence of Waterford in 1948 hadn't the same impact because it had always been deemed a hurling county.

Incidentally, some of the traditionalists looked on Offaly's great achievement as some kind of freak happening; I heard them called 'scoopers'. This word probably comes from scuaibín, the name given to cross-country hurling, the counterpart of Caid.

Television has given a great boost to the ancient game – and so, of course, has the coming of headgear. It is such a good idea that you wonder why it wasn't adopted long ago.

I know of no game that arouses more passion than hurling and I know of no game that evokes more dedication in its exponents; around it there is a kind of healthy madness, fiabhras na fuinseoige. Imprinted on my mind there are three images that tell a lot about the game.

I see Lory Meagher putting a ladder up against a cock of hay and going back about fifty yards and pucking a sliotar under the bottom rung – and pucking another under the next rung, and so on – and sometimes starting again until he had got it all right.

When Christy Ring drove an oil lorry around the roads of Cork, he kept a hurley and a bucket of sliotars in his cab; the bucket was flattened on one side; he put it down in a field during his lunch hour – that was his target.

Then there was the occasion when Galway, long out of the centre court, were on the way to winning the Final of the League. The three Connolly brothers, natives of Connemara, were on board. Mícheál Ó'Muircheartaigh broke into Gaelic and delivered the last twelve minutes of his commentary in the old tongue.

We all love to speculate about who was the greatest hurler of all time – it is good and endless fun. I prefer to name the man who for me most symbolises all that is great in the game. He is Tony Doran, The Happy Warrior.

Brendan Fullam has gone into the forest that he has so long loved and that he knows so well and brought back great stories. Mo bheannacht.

* Legends of The Ash is published by Wolfhound Press.

Sunday World, October 19, 1997

Ladies reach untold heights

About half-past two on Sunday I was in the cavern under the Hogan Stand and experienced a heart-warming spectacle: about thirty young girls in Blue-and-Gold were embracing in a wild circle and chanting: "Campiones, Campiones, Campiones. Olé, Olé, Olé".

This was a nice example of how cultures influence one another. Longford had just won the All-Ireland Junior Football final; it was the County's first.

It is a long time since the heart of the Midlands has been in the sporting headlines, not since Brendan Barden and his merry men won the National League in 1966. That was a great team: they might have won the All-Ireland if they hadn't shown Kerry too much respect in the Semi-Final.

That was in 1968. Longford made a woeful start but made a marvellous recovery and lost by only two points. The victory of the girls was all the sweeter after that long absence; the celebrations were ecstatic. Longford beat Tyrone by 2-12 to 1-11.

Thus they completed The League and Championship double. Next season they will be in the Senior ranks. Monaghan and Waterford sent out a message on Sunday that it will take a very good team to displace them from the upper branches of the tree.

In the Senior game we saw in fair degree of skill and a high level of fitness. I have missed only one Final since the first in 1974; in 1991 I had to cover the Finals of the World Cup in Rugby - Sunday's game was the only one that ended in controversy.

The second half lasted for more than eleven minutes beyond normal time. This was a record for any game that I've ever seen in Hurling or Gaelic Football or Ladies' Football.

That stint of broken time seemed unreal: as it went on and on, I got a crazy idea that perhaps there was a new rule to get rid of a draw and that we were waiting for a clinching score - as in the Final of The Euro Cup last year.

I might as well add that I hadn't a watch; I was depending on the clock above The Canal Terrace; this is hardly a precise chronometer - a colleague who was better equipped told me that the broken time extended to 11 minutes and 52 seconds.

I am sure that there is a full video of the game; it would be interesting to find out how much time was lost. There should be an independent timekeeper. This problem is not new: in The Hurling Final in 1996 full time was not played.

It was a pity that even the slightest smidgeon of controversy should be attached to this Final - it was a memorable game. I wouldn't call it great because the first half was too one-sided - the second compensated in excitement and eventually in drama.

This final will be remembered for many reasons, most of all perhaps for the display of Edel Byrne - it was a day of magic for the sprite from Magheracloone, a townland near Carrickmacross.

It is a resounding name and, as far as I know, it means The Meadow On The Plain. I might as well add that the five saintly people who are running for The Park needn't bother to ask Edel for her vote - she is only fifteen.

I know many able girls who have tried and tried for long and laborious years to win All-Ireland Gold; Edel has achieved it in her first season as a Senior - I can hear my friend Jason Sherlock laughing to himself.

Seemingly Waterford won the toss and chose to play into the wind and the Railway Goal. They may have regretted their choice as Monaghan made a brilliant start that was crowned with a goal in the 10th minute.

As a ball bounced about ten yards from Waterford's citadel, it became a race between the keeper, Annalisa Crotty, and Edel - the forward got her hands to it and it rolled into the net.

Waterford compensated within a few minutes: a long high ball from Geraldine O'Ryan deceived friend and foe and floated into the net. The best goal came in the 22nd minute.

An attack began in midfield; almost inevitably young Miss Byrne had a hand; she gave the final pass to Niamh Kindlon who found a small parcel of space about 18 yards from goal and gave the keeper little chance.

Monaghan led by 2-9 to 1-3 at the break; I was almost certain that the contest was over. Waterford would now have the wind; it was breathing diagonally from the Nally Stand and didn't seem of great significance.

Perhaps its effect was mainly in the mind; for whatever reason, Waterford now began to show why they have been such a dominant force since Kerry won their fabulous nine in a row between 1982 and 1990.

Their revival resembled that of Mayo against Kerry in the recent final; there was a difference - they were translating their territorial superiority into scores.

Geraldine O'Ryan put Monaghan a point ahead in the 59th minute; their followers began to cheer them home but play went on and on in broken time and Jenny Greenan equalised in the 65th minute.

Most people expected Mr Finbarr O'Driscoll to signal full time but play went on - and when Edel put Monaghan ahead with a point, hundreds invaded the pitch.

It was cleared with little difficulty. Edel added another point. Now Waterford's case seemed hopeless; they needed a goal and obviously there could be only seconds left.

However, the final drama was to come; a long low ball went behind the back three and ran to Mary O'Donnell, in the middle and thirty yards from goal; she lost a precious fraction of time in picking it up and the posse cut her off at the pass.

Thus it all ended at 2-15 to 1-16. Most of the Waterford girls were almost inconsolable.

Jenny Greenan and Linda Farrelly gave Monaghan midfield dominance in the first half; Martina O'Ryan and Noreen Walsh compensated in the second. Angela Larkin was Monaghan's leading forward; Geraldine O'Ryan was her counterpart.

This game emphasised two truths for me: the first is rather obvious; although soccer has penetrated into almost every nook and cranny in this island since the televised World Cup Finals in 1966, it has had little effect on Gaelic Football or on Ladies' Football.

The other truth may not be so obvious. It concerns the pick-up. The girls may pick up with their hands but there are times when a clean lift with the foot would be more profitable - some day some coach will see this.

Over 15,000 paid into Croke Park on Sunday. The attendance is growing year by year. The best is yet to be.

Friday, May 26, 1989

Requiem for a sad hero

A few years ago the syndicated American columnist, Jim Murray, wrote out a list of things that it would be better you didn't see.

They included a great ship going down, a wounded lion surrounded by jackals —and Joe Louis in a wheelchair.

The famous columnist had just been to Las Vegas and seen the great champion in Caesar's Palace, physically stricken and mentally clouded.

What deepened the tragedy was that Joe had brought his troubles on himself.

A recently-published book* written by his son Joe Louis Barrow in conjunction with Barbara Munder delineates Joe's decline unsentimentally.

I suppose you could say he was the ultimate example of a great athlete who found life intolerable when his sporting career was over.

And it is probably true to say that the greater the peak, the more difficult it is to settle in the plain.

Most of us know footballers and hurlers who are still playing epic games long after they have stowed the camán and the boots in the cubby under the stairs

Most of these day-dreamers come to little harm – but the world heavyweight championship is sport's greatest honour; Joe Louis had a long way to come down.

The public image of him as ending up as a greeter in Caesar's Palace isn't quite accurate.

He was still very much of a celebrity; people liked to meet him; they could go home and tell their friends about what they had said to Joe Louis and what he had said to them.

Joe, like a great many American blacks, loved to gamble – and so Las Vegas suited him down to the ground and sometimes up to the sky.

Seemingly in his rather strange profession he had no fixed wages – he played it by ear.

This in loose translation meant that when he was broke – which was fairly often – he went to the boss for some money.

His spiel was simple: "It don't look too good for the heavyweight champion of the world to walk around busted – I think you had better give me a couple of hundred."

His boss, Ash Resnick, though a casino owner was a decent man; Joe didn't walk around busted too often.

Gambling was his chief method of parting with money; he didn't touch alcohol in those days – and, as everyone knows, you can drink only so much but you can gamble any amount.

Joe, as you have probably guessed by now, wouldn't dream of quitting while he was ahead – and inevitably almost always ended up a loser.

One day he was so many thousand dollars ahead at blackjack that Resnick wished to put some of it away for him – Joe declined.

A few hours later he came to the boss and explained that it didn't look well for a great champion to walk around busted.

When Joe first came to Las Vagas, he loved the excitement and the adulation but eventually he began to be weary of it all.

He turned to drugs: he remembered the year, the day of the month, the hour and even the number of the hotel bedroom where he was introduced to cocaine.

Some time later he tasted alcohol for the first time in his life: cocaine and Courvoisier made a potent cocktail.

Joe was on the downward slope; his mind began to go; he behaved irrationally; he became so suspicious that people were out to kill him that he wouldn't eat unless someone first tasted the food.

The irony of it all was that he had no enemy except himself; very few of his old friends deserted him; Frank Sinatra and Billy Conn proved especially considerate.

There was little that they could do – like the man in William Cowper's poem, he was out of humanity's reach.

He died on April 12, 1981. There was some doubt about his age. Not all sharecroppers' children are registered at birth; he was about sixty-five.

Many people who are deemed expert regard Joe Louis as the greatest heavyweight of all time; of course it is a subjective matter but there is an abundance of evidence on their side.

There is an inscription to him in Madison Square Garden which almost amounts to canonisation.

And he received a very rare honour, The Army's Distinguished Service Medal, the highest award that The Army can confer on a civilian.

What not everybody may know is that Joe had a great sense of humour; not for nothing was he an American black – humour is the anodyne of the oppressed.

And he was no slouch on the verbal draw, as Muhammad Ali found out.

One day when Louis was having lunch with some friends, Ali joined them uninvited and explained the ploys he would have used to beat him if their careers had coincided.

Joe listened quietly and when at last the stream of words ceased, he said: "Listen boy – if you only dream about it, you should apologise."

Ali, as the world knows, idolised Louis, studied his films intensely, and based some of his tactics on him – and, incidentally, was very good to him in the grey years.

Ali's own decline may have a specific medical cause but you cannot help wondering if it isn't mentally conditioned.

Joe's first wife, Marva, summarised his troubles in words that seem just as relevant to Ali.

"Joe was on a roller-coaster. He couldn't stand still. He always had to be moving. I think the end of the adulation was responsible for his final breakdown."

Joe was born in The Deepest South, spent his boyhood in Detroit – and the best of his boxing years in New York or thereabouts.

And of course he was adored in Harlem – we tend to forget that he was only the second black champion.

One evening recently I went to see that famous – or notorious – quarter and was surprised.

I had thought of it as a slumland; maybe it is but it doesn't look the part; it has just about the finest streets in Manhattan, wide and tree-lined.

And for good or bad measure it adjoins that marvellous rectangle of wood and water and hills and hollows known as Central Park. There is a catch – most of Harlem's citizens live in high rises.

*'The Brown Bomber' is published by Arthur Barker at £12.95 sterling.

The Sunday World, May 31

The Cockney Boy

Few Irish people go to The Derby: Epsom seems to be a distant third in their priorities to Cheltenham and Aintree - and yet I believe that at least one visit to The Downs should be part of a liberal education.

It is very easy to get to Epsom: it is only twenty miles from the heart of London; there is a great train service from Waterloo and Victoria - and buses meet the trains at Epsom station.

It is a wonderful experience to be part of about half-a-million people in the one field, if you can call it a field - it is a vast rolling common. I have been there on many occasions - but whenever I go, it always seems to be the first time.

There was an occasion when I wasn't there but that nevertheless produced a famous story; it wasn't altogether my fault - it all happened some time late in the nineteenth century. The central characters were a publican and his potboy and a horse.

The publican loved racing and eventually decided that he could afford to be a player rather than a spectator - and so, abetted by his potboy, he went to a sale and purchased a two-year-old, so well bred that he could run in The Derby.

The colt was brought to the yard behind the public house and comfortably stabled; he was almost certainly the first racehorse ever to be lodged in The Mile End Road; he was given a name - The Cockney Boy.

The publican had no land but there was a common close by; it was called London Fields - it still is. I know it: a counterpart of Phoenix Park it is not but it served as a training ground for The Cockney Boy.

The potboy was a jockey who had fallen on hard times but he had retained his licence; he educated the young hopeful; he wasn't raced as a two-year-old - he was aimed for The Derby.

His appearance in London Fields fascinated the good people of The East End and indeed most parts of working-class London - here was a colt with an aristocratic background.

He stood out in a world of horses and cobs and ponies that had been sentenced to spend their lives pulling drays or milkcarts or breadvans or whatever.

There was a whiff of revolution in the air: a colt from the world of the common people would challenge for the great prize that had long been the precluse of ignoble lords and robber barons.

Crowds gathered to watch the colt and the faithful potboy as they went about their preparations; the fascination grew as the big day approached - working-class London was agog.

There were no betting shops in those days but there was no lack of people, mostly publicans, who were willing to take a wager. The people of The East End had infinite faith in the local hero - biscuit tins and old stockings and piggybanks were raided.

And on a glorious June morning there was an almighty exodus to the south. The Downs had never housed such a multitude. People came from all walks and stumbles of life and from almost every part of London.

They came from Millwall and Hackney and Hoxton and Spitalfields and Bethnal Green and The Isle Of Dogs - I could go on and on. An elderly couple set out from Islington but they dallied at a pie shop in Fleet Street and missed the last train from Waterloo.

Meanwhile below in The Downs you could see the common people, many of them in their native dress, already celebrating the victory over their alleged superiors.

The Fall of The Bastille would seem no more than a footnote to history compared to the sight of the colt from The East End storming up the hill from Tattenham Corner with his rivals floundering behind.

As half-past three drew nigh, the atmosphere was almost unbearable; some people were even driven to drink to calm themselves down. The Cockney Boy couldn't but be affected by the medley of sights and sounds and smells.

The potboy had to lead him down to the start and he didn't get on board until the last possible moment and then he kept his pupil behind a wall of horses.

Alas, after about three furlongs a gap opened and the poor horse bolted and crashed through the outside rail and scattered the crowd assembled near Tattenham Corner. It was a miracle that nobody was seriously injured - it was no more than a case of broken bones.

The Cockney Boy was found next morning, wandering in a field near Walton-on-the-Hill. The potboy didn't come back to London for several days. It was a sad end to what began as a romantic story.

Sunday World, October 19, 1997

A great newspaper man

I shared one of the most memorable occasions of my life with Shane Flynn. It was in the stewardship of Eoin Hand. The date was the 9th of September, 1981. The place was Rotterdam. The game was in the qualifying round for the World Cup.

We came from behind twice and got a famous draw against a great Dutch team. Shane and I got involved with our team in the celebrations and missed the coach back to the hotel; we stowed away on a milk train and got back to Amsterdam at about three o'clock.

When we got to our hotel in the Old Quarter, a party was getting up a great head of steam. It was an occasion when The Noble Call proliferated - when somebody finished his act, he nominated his successor.

My turn came. I sang The Ballad of Joe Hill. Then of course I nominated Shane. He performed his famous imitation of Brendan Grace's Bottler. We saw the dawn come up over The Rhine.

Then there was the dramatic semi-final in 1977 when Dublin shattered Kerry with an amazing scoreburst in the last ten minutes. Whenever I began to boast about The Kingdom's prowess, Shane had only to mention the year - for him it was a talisman.

I have never known a braver person: for about ten years he suffered from a recurring illness but I never heard him complain - he got on with his life; his zest was never diminished. Such was his appetite for work that he was at his desk until a few weeks before he departed this world.

Shane was basically a sub-editor - and a good one; he also wrote regularly for GAA publications - and he wrote well. I loved his weekly column in the Evening Press - it was called Paper Talk.

It was a light-hearted distillation of the great little papers that are published late on Saturdays in our neighbouring island; they deal mainly with football - and in the trade they are known as The Pinks.

I never thought of Shane either as a sub-editor or as a writer: to me he was quintessentially a newspaper man; I never knew anyone as much in love with the craft and with the good ship Irish Press.

He knew everything that went on in Burgh Quay; he was as intimate with the old building as Robin Hood and Maid Marion and Friar Tuck and Will Scarlett were with the glades and dells of Sherwood Forest. By comparison I was a stranger in the house.

Shane, behind the image of the laughing boy, was a very serious person and a great trade unionist. He was the hero of that black week-end in late July of 1990 when our good ship seemed about to sink.

He was the main organiser of the meeting that brought us back from the brink. For that I would forgive him anything, even his devotion to Rangers; whenever I went to Glasgow to watch one of their clashes with Celtic, I brought him back a programme.

I was privileged to know Shane for over twenty years as a colleague and as a friend; we did a fair amount of work together - and "we heard the chimes at midnight".